ACCULTURATED

Acculturated

Edited by Naomi Schaefer Riley
and Christine Rosen

TEMPLETON PRESS

Templeton Press
300 Conshohocken State Road, Suite 550
West Conshohocken, PA 19428
www.templetonpress.org

© 2011 by Templeton Press

Designed and typeset by Gopa and Ted2, Inc.

Library of Congress Cataloging-in-Publication Data

Acculturated / edited by Naomi Schaefer Riley and Christine Rosen.
       p. cm.
   ISBN-13: 978-1-59947-372-7 (hardback : alk. paper)
   ISBN-10: 1-59947-372-0 (hardback : alk. paper) 1. Mass media and culture—United States. 2. Popular culture—United States.
I. Riley, Naomi Schaefer. II. Rosen, Christine, 1973-
   P94.65.U6.A28 2011
   302.23—dc22

                                        2010051913

Printed in the United States of America

11   12 13   14   15   16   10 9 8 7 6 5 4 3 2 1

Contents

Introduction

Naomi Schaefer Riley and Christine Rosen

MYTHS. LEGENDS. Bible stories. Fairy tales. Fables. Every culture in every era finds a way to express our human need to tell stories about ourselves. We rely on these stories to teach us why we do the things we do, to test the limits of our experience, and to reaffirm deeply felt truths about human nature. They are the explicit and implicit vehicles for teaching younger generations about vice and virtue, honor and shame, and a great deal more.

The contemporary crop of reality television shows, with their bevy of "real housewives," super-size families, and toddler beauty-pageant candidates, seems an unlikely place to find truths about human nature or examples of virtue. And yet on these shows, and in much else of what passes for popular culture these days, a surprising theme emerges: move beyond the visual excess and hyperbole and you will find the makings of classic morality tales. Bad characters come to disastrous ends; people struggle with unexpected hardship and either triumph or fail, depending on their strength of character. For some, hard work pays off. For others, failure is swift and cruel. All of these dramas play to a large and eager audience of viewers.

Americans increasingly understand their own reality through the prism of these television shows and the celebrity-industrial complex they support. Indeed, for many Americans, and particularly for younger Americans, popular culture *is* culture, for it is the only kind of cultural experience they seek and the currency in which they trade. Whether through television, movies, tabloid magazine or websites, blogs, social-networking sites, and video-sharing sites such as YouTube, the public now has unparalleled opportunities to observe, comment on, and create popular culture. Our new technologies give us a steady diet of images and information, right down to the eating, dressing, and mating habits of every would-be celebrity in the world.

Liberal-minded observers tend to praise the smashing of taboos and anything-goes extremism of pop culture. Conservatives tend to tut-tut about declining standards and moral relativism. What is missing from the landscape of cultural criticism is a sustained and thoughtful discussion about what popular culture has to teach us about ourselves—our values, our interests, and our hopes for the future—and the ways in which we might reclaim some space in popular culture for a discussion of things such as virtue and character. Popular culture tackles the full spectrum of human experience: birth, death, love, marriage, hatred, failure, and redemption. Although commentary on popular culture often focuses on the multitude of settings where virtue and character are absent, might it also be possible to create cultural settings that could encourage things such as thrift, compassion, and self-reliance?

These are some of the questions we tackle in this book. The title *Acculturated* is a play on words: although the essays in this volume are steeped in the culture and aware of the current trends in a variety of media, the book is also "A Culture Rated"—that is, our contributors have taken a step or two back from the unceasing din of popular culture so that they might better judge its values and help readers think more deeply about what the barrage of narratives around them really mean.

The book is organized thematically into four sections: The first section explores relationships and the myriad and often contradictory ways popular culture teaches us how to behave, how to treat each other, and, for better and for worse, how well we are learning these lessons. The second section of the book explores the world of children and teen culture. Kids are perhaps the most avid consumers of and market for pop culture. What does our current culture reflect about their experiences, from Facebook friendship to Lady Gaga metamorphoses to the often-chilling yet wildly popular narratives of teenage fiction? The third section of the book examines some of the surprising and counterintuitive ways pop culture has changed the way we spend our leisure time, whether watching professional sports or playing video games. The last section tackles that most American of pursuits: self-improvement. Whether we are learning how to cook, going back to school, or just trying to lose a few pounds, pop culture has a reality television show or blog chronicling others' experiences. What does our avid vicarious consumption of others' struggles tell us about ourselves?

Perhaps no other forum in popular culture today offers us greater access to others' lives than reality television. When did reality television start? Some observers trace it to a documentary called *An American Family*, the story of a nuclear family going through a divorce, which aired on PBS in the 1970s. Others point to *The Real World*, MTV's portrayal of a new group of young people thrown together in a group house in a different city every year, which has been on the air for nearly two decades. But there is a good argument for placing *The Dating Game* at the start of the reality TV trend. With both "real people" and occasional appearances by singers and actors, *The Dating Game* reflected much about the state of romantic relationships and the relationship of ordinary people to celebrities in the late twentieth century.

In a 1972 episode now archived on YouTube, a young Michael Jackson—he had just turned fourteen—was the show's bachelor, interviewing three obviously happy, but nonetheless composed and polite adolescent girls. The three adorably dressed fans—one had never missed a day of school, another starred in her school play, and the final contestant liked both tap and modern dance—kept their answers short. No one spoke out of turn. The meanest thing in the episode was one girl's admission that she thought another contestant resembled Mickey Mouse. When Jackson asked one of the young women to describe what she thought it would be like to share a kiss with him, she smiles sweetly and says, "Lovely."

At the time the episode aired, Michael Jackson had the number one selling album in the country. It's a little hard to imagine this scene repeated today with Usher, the Jonas Brothers, or Justin Bieber. The reason is not simply that there are no sweet, innocent thirteen-year-old girls left. It's because our relationships—particularly ones with the opposite sex—are now filtered through the prism of popular culture. The girls who were being courted by Michael Jackson were behaving the way they were taught to in ordinary life. One doesn't imagine their answers would be much different if a young suitor was sitting with them at a dinner table and their extended families were all present.

Today, the girls would likely adopt a television persona to better suit our more revealing and consciously therapeutic times. One-word answers would be replaced by long sentences of self-conscious observations about how excited they are to be there and how worried they are about their appearance or their answers. If one of them still seemed nice at the end of the episode, that person would be "the nice one." More likely they would all be shrieking or offering up risqué responses to titillate the audience.

It is not just television; the Internet has also had this effect on our relationships. We think about ourselves differently and we present ourselves to others differently, too. As Megan Basham writes in her essay regarding online dating: "The idea that what people write on their Facebook profiles or answer in personality questionnaires is a perfect reflection of who they actually are is demonstrably naive. It can just as easily reflect who they want to be or whom they want others to think they are more than it does the true person. That goes doubly for the young." Basham even acknowledges: "If I'd had a Facebook page in my late teens and early twenties, I probably would have posted pictures and links that made me look flirtatious, impulsive, and carefree because at the time it's who I aspired to be."

And yet, popular culture doesn't always urge us to perform our worst versions of ourselves. In fact, it often reminds us of the boundaries we must not cross in our real-life relationships. As Kay Hymowitz notes in her essay on adultery, we may think we live in an anything-goes world, but the taboo against adultery remains as strong as ever. And the prohibition is beaten into us at every opportunity in what Hymowitz terms a National Adultery Ritual: "A politician or role model is discovered to have betrayed his wife with another woman, or as it frequently happens, women. The press circles and the shame fest begins. The sinner is subjected to a veritable waterboarding of late-night TV jokes, derisive cartoons, tabloid headlines, embarrassing interviews with the mistress and other former girlfriends, analyses by psychologists on the inner demons that drove the man to such behavior, rampant speculation on the future of the bleeding marriage . . . a sane person might prefer a scarlet letter."

Beyond serving as morality tales, what do celebrity relationships and our relationships with celebrities do to us? We gawk, we imitate, we cringe. But we also wonder how our own lives would look on TV, on the Internet, and in the movies. What would the viewers say about us right now, for instance?

Before reality television and social-networking sites, the public could easily distinguish between real people and glamorous actors. No one's marriage really looked like Donna Reed's or Dick Van Dyke's or Bill Cosby's sitcom marriage. But now, we're not so sure. We can all be actors. We can all be celebrities. Maybe that couple on the screen really does have amazing sex every night. Maybe they really do know how to balance work and family and throw great dinner parties and raise wonderful children too. And before you know it, we're looking at our spouse and wondering, "Why can't we be like that, honey?"

Pop culture is capable of criticizing that urge as easily as it celebrates it. The recent film *The Joneses*, starring Demi Moore and David Duchovny, follows the diabolically clever careers of four people who work for a stealth marketing company. Posing as the perfect family, they infiltrate upper-class neighborhoods and impress their peers with their remarkable lifestyle—all with the intent of selling people things they don't need and can't afford. The fake family's denouement is a far more compelling critique of American materialism (and argument for thrift) than any earnest documentary about overspending could be.

As well, we tend to forget how much television, e-mail, blogs, Twitter, and social-networking sites have influenced our perceptions of time. We are quick to admit that we have more difficulty focusing for long periods of time and can't get through a long book any more. But what about the instant gratification of getting a note back from someone, of being able to tell everyone what you're doing all the time, of watching whatever show you want to whenever you want? These can help relationships thrive just us easily as they can harm them.

Where pop culture often falls short is in relaying the message that there are certain habits that can only be mastered through repetition and extensive practice; there are qualities—virtues even—that cannot be developed in the time it takes to blog about them. Children don't have a good grasp on time, and popular culture does them a disservice when it suggests that everything can happen overnight. The unpopular can become popular. The ugly can become beautiful. The single become attached. Even a show like *Made* on MTV, which helps teens "achieve their dreams" of becoming homecoming queen, losing weight, earning a spot in the school play—all projects that take months—can be viewed in an afternoon. The transformation can seem instantaneous, at least to the viewer.

And teens, more than ever, are surrounded by "nowness." With their own smartphones and laptops and televisions, their worlds are whittled down to their immediate concerns. As Mark Bauerlein writes, teen culture "raises ordinary fears and ambitions of the teen ego—Do I look okay? Do they like me? Am I invited? Can I get a car?—to dramatic, decisive standing. The very presence of youth on twelve different channels for hours every day and night grants a lasting validity and consequence to youth aims and anxieties even when the outcomes of the plots display their shortsightedness." To the extent that adults are present in this teen world, they are observers, sometimes even puppeteers, trying to manipulate the children. As Caitlin Flanagan describes in her essay on the young-adult book series, *The Hunger Games*, teens in fiction are often pitted against one another in a struggle to survive. But it is all done for the entertainment of the adults.

Adults spend a large percentage of their leisure time consuming pop culture as well. For many of them, the immediacy and impermanence of pop culture is also part of its allure. Shows that fail to garner an audience quickly disappear. And pop culture's insatiable appetite for the newest thing allows for endless reinvention: yesterday's sitcom has-been is today's *Dancing with the Stars* contestant, and today's reality television show contestant is tomorrow's cohost of *The View*.

But impatience also exacts a price: it erodes our ability to appreciate things that take time, whether that is developing a friendship or mastering a hobby. As Megan McArdle details in her essay on cooking culture, time is the enemy of most modern cooks, and so, inspired by cooking shows and celebrity chefs, they spend their money creating perfect kitchens and turning out showy meals but not their time making everyday food for their loved ones. "For all the tongue-clucking about obesity that you often hear from upper middle-class foodies," McArdle notes, "I wonder if we middle-class aspirational chefs aren't the worst gluttons of all. When we are alone, we eat almost furtively . . . and when we are with others, we cannot simply delight in feeding our friends.

We must overwhelm them with our food—no, not with our food, but with our marvelous, marvelous selves."

Then again, contemporary pop culture also offers new, positive opportunities for socializing, as Jonathan Last describes in his essay on social video games such as Wii bowling. He finds it encouraging that "after years of tearing at the social fabric, the video game has once again become part of the tapestry of American sociability, another thread that helps bind us together." Similarly, Wilfred McClay mines the great American songbook of the twentieth century and finds inspiration for twenty-first-century popular music. "As the form flourished," McClay writes, about songs such as those by Cole Porter and the Gershwins, "it gave expression to an ethos, one to which I think we can profitably return—not to wallow in it nostalgically, or readopt it anachronistically, but to learn something from it about the art of living."

It is the art of living, and, broadly speaking, the American art of self-improvement that provide the theme of the essays in the final section of the book. Patrick Allitt describes Americans' enthusiasm for lifelong learning through the lens of businesses like the Teaching Company, which sells lectures on a wide array of subjects to an eager audience of American self-improvers. Judy Bachrach offers suggestions for how pop culture, particularly television and film, might better portray the realities of death and dying since today, as she observes, "The death you see on the screen will not be the death you have." Chuck Colson tackles the subject of forgiveness by asking what contemporary culture deems sinful. "A society that doesn't take sin seriously has difficulty taking forgiveness seriously," Colson argues. "After all, if nobody does anything wrong, there's nothing to forgive."

Contemporary popular culture, from books to film to television to music, has provoked a great deal of criticism, some of it well deserved. But for better or worse, popular culture *is* culture and it serves an increasingly important function in Americans' everyday lives. It is not just an escape from everyday life; it is a commentary on it as well. It is a tool that we use to create better lives for ourselves and our children, whether our aspirations are as mundane as losing a little weight or as ambitious as forgiving our mortal enemies. Much like a mirror, popular culture reflects what our society looks like: brash, ambitious, at times vulgar, but also capable of generosity, self-improvement, and honesty. If we don't like what we see in the mirror of pop culture, we do have the power to change it. This book is a modest attempt to do just that. By bringing together an eclectic range of contributors who raise provocative questions about pop culture, we hope to encourage a debate about its meaning in contemporary life and offer some suggestions for the way forward.

Part 1

Love in a Time of Reality TV

1: Sex, Lies, and YouTube

Kay S. Hymowitz

IF THE HEADLINES seem to tell us one thing about our culture, it is that we are living in the Age of Adultery. A steady line of prominent men have taken the walk of shame across our television screens and through our magazine and newspaper pages over the past decade or so; Bill Clinton (he says it wasn't sex, but would even he deny it was adultery?), Newt Gingrich, Rudy Giuliani, the three Johns (Edwards, Ensign, and Gosselin), Jim McGreevy, Mark Sanford, Eliot Spitzer, and Tiger Woods. These are just the thirty-minutes-of-fame-ers. There are plenty of other minor-league cads who got their more commonly apportioned fifteen minutes—San Francisco mayor Gavin Newsom, CNN legal analyst Jeffrey Toobin (said to have fathered the child of Casey Greenfield, daughter of pundit eminence Jeff Greenfield), eight-term Indiana congressman Mark Souder; no doubt by the time these words reach print, there will be others. Add them all together, and culture and politics seem like they're all adultery, all the time.

To many observers, the problem is not so much the lapses of the men in question as the public obsession with them. Why, they ask, are the media and its consumers so preoccupied with these matters when we have so many important things to be pondering? Why are we chattering about sex tapes and cigars when there are loose nukes and economic mayhem out there? These objections frequently come with accusations against a corporate media interested only in profit and indifferent to the public welfare. At any rate, sexual relationships are private, aren't they?

Actually, no. In this bloggy, YouTube, and memoir-flooded era, people describe grazing the sexual buffet with little shame or embarrassment; oral, anal, threesomes, hookups, dildos, hand-cuffs, whips, vibrators, or whatever else floats your boat. Adultery is one exception to this open-mindedness, especially when it involves powerful men in the public eye. If they cheat on their wives, those men will be facing the pursed lips and wagging fingers of Americans, and particularly women, in high moral dudgeon.

Of course, though it is a flashpoint, adultery is hardly taboo. Dating websites for cheaters appear on the Internet and no one is trying to shut them down. In fact, the most famous of them, AshleyMadison.com, cheekily urges, "Life is Short: Have an Affair." As for cheating celebrities, we tend to go easy on them, probably because they exist in a different realm than the rest of us; they are more like bickering Olympian gods and goddesses than ordinary bottom-dwellers like ourselves.

But male—they are almost always male for reasons that will become clear—politicians and role models? They're going to suffer for their adulterous ways. In fact, they will be put through what might be called the National Adultery Ritual. A politician, or in Woods's case, a role model and a valuable corporate brand, is discovered to have betrayed his wife with another woman, or as it frequently happens, women. The press circles and the shame fest begins. The sinner is subjected to a veritable waterboarding of late-night TV jokes, derisive cartoons, tabloid headlines, embarrassing interviews with the mistress and other former girlfriends, analyses by psychologists on the inner demons that drove the man to such behavior, rampant speculation on the future of the bleeding marriage. Then there are the car and helicopter chases, flashing cameras, the gawkers, the plague of paparazzi locusts and microphones, and countless replaying of all of this on YouTube: a sane person might prefer a scarlet letter.

Consider the public judgment rendered on Mark Sanford, cheating husband of Jenny Sanford, father of four Sanford sons, and officially censured governor of South Carolina. The term "laughingstock" comes from the medieval tradition of clamping a malefactor in wooden leg and arm restraints in the town square where passersby could jeer and throw things at his helpless form. Sanford was the twenty-first-century man in the stocks. Television hosts mocked him mercilessly. David Letterman (at the time an undisclosed adulterer, although as an entertainer more easily forgiven) tried this: "Governor Mark Sanford disappeared . . . and it turned out he was in South America. And then it turned out he was down there because he was sleeping with a woman from Argentina. Once again, foreigners taking jobs that Americans won't do." Keith Olbermann labeled Sanford the "Wild Bull of the Pampas" and provided a dramatic reading of his e-mails with schmaltzy mood music playing in the background, lingering lasciviously over the parts about the curve of his lover's hips and her hidden tan lines.

Nor are professional comics and pundits the only ones to enjoy debasing the sinner. When given the chance, the public eagerly joins in. After Tiger Woods's wrongdoing came to light, amateur preachers took to YouTube. "Tiger 'n Whores" was one musical contribution to the golfer's punishment; "They're both pros at what they do," goes one of the lines. Another preacher mocking the golfer's dubious taste in mistresses called his video: "Tiger Woods: You Are a Man Whore!" CNN's story about the Sanford divorce was followed by angry verbal rock-throwing from commenters: "scumbag," "dweeb," "dirtbag," they scrawled. "Go crawl under a rock. Oh and keep your mouth shut because everything that comes out of it is a LIE!!!"

If details of the affair in question come to light, the public uses them to further humiliate the adulterer. Details strip the sinner of any remaining dignity by undermining his intact selfhood and effectively giving the public the ammunition to say: "We own you now!" The most dangerous moment for Bill Clinton was always the cigar and the blue dress, and not just because the latter provided legal evidence. They fleshed out our mental picture of the president during moments no one should have known about, and giving each of us power over a man who knows us not at all.

The case of Sanford's fellow "love-guv," former New York chief executive Eliot Spitzer who was caught consorting with prostitutes, yielded a mother lode of prurient detail with which to ridicule the malefactor: he liked rough sex, with his socks on and condom off; he was Client 9 at the Emperor's Club; he was a "difficult customer." *New York* magazine put his picture on its cover; its caption read "brain" with an arrow pointing toward his misbehaving privates. It was a nasty barb, but a pinprick compared to a cringe-making *Vanity Fair* cartoon portraying a naked female receiving money from a leering Spitzer, also naked—except for his long black socks.

This torrent of mockery is bad enough, but the adulterer must still undergo the press conference, the ritual's climactic moment. During this weird event, the cornered sinner must confess, and he must do so in a very particular fashion. Resignation from office is optional, but grim-faced apology is not. By now everyone knows the liturgy by heart: I have disappointed those I care most deeply about, I have no one to blame but myself, I ask that you please respect the privacy of my family, etc. Sanford was ruined once he went off script; instead of asking for forgiveness from his family and his constituents, he rambled on about his soulmate.

Despite its formulaic nature, the press conference has an important purpose: specifically to convince the public of the sinner's sincerity, and more generally to probe his character. The truth is people are willing to forgive. They know sex can make a fool of just about anyone under the right circumstances, and they suspect that powerful men confront many temptations. But to gain public forgiveness the sinner must be really truly sorry, not just to have been caught, but to have had sex with other wom(e)n. He must show he is capable of genuine remorse, something that the unalloyed villain is not. During the unfolding of the Edwards scandal, *People* ran an article entitled "Marriage Betrayal: When Apologies Don't Cut It" with quotes from the press conferences of Edwards, Bill Clinton, and an assortment of cheating celebrities. The article included a poll asking readers to vote: "Who sounds most sincere?" but the editors were not simply asking for an evaluation of a performance. They were asking, "Who can be trusted?"

Spitzer's signs of remorse were heartfelt enough that within nine months of his press conference, the ex-governor was poking his head out of his private bunker, writing a biweekly column for the online magazine *Slate*, and appearing on television news shows. He eventually scored his own show, with cohost Kathleen Parker, on CNN. How did he do it? Spitzer moved quickly to meet with the media and he was brief and to the point. He had "begun to atone for his private failings," he said, but he recognized his betrayal of the public. He resigned from office, giving the impression he was ready to put his ambition on hold and engage in the necessary inner struggle. His wife's demeanor, described by the press as "ashen-faced" and "stricken," provided a shocking display of genuine emotion in the midst of the predictable ceremony. The first sightings of the penitent ex-governor after his resignation also helped: he was spotted taking his dog for a walk, waving good-bye to his eldest daughter as she set out to school, getting in the minivan with his wife, two younger kids, and two dogs for a family weekend. His classy wife's apparent forgiveness added to his rehabilitation. Spitzer's case was unusual, however, because of a lucky (for him) financial crisis. Not only did this former "Sheriff of Wall Street" look prescient, but the industry's sleaze took our attention off his.

John Edwards was the opposite of the genuine repentant. He not only refused to come clean, but he also lied about the extent of his affair and his paternity of his mistress's baby. Clinging to his ambitions, he tried a preposterous cover-up—having an aide claim to be the father—thereby figuratively doing to his staff and supporters what he had literally done to his mistress. Worse, his previously admired wife joined in the sham. According to political reporters John Heileman and Mark Halperin, in their best-selling book *Game Change*, during his career people often reacted to Edwards as "a pretty boy phony"—until they saw Elizabeth, plump and four years his senior. Before the scandal, Elizabeth had lent John depth and authenticity; a handsome, successful man like the senator from North Carolina could have any beauty queen he wanted, but he had chosen a weight-struggling everywoman. But her Lady Macbeth ambition destroyed her image. "[B]ecause of a picture falsely suggesting that John was spending time with a child it wrongly alleged he had fathered outside our marriage," Elizabeth fibbed in August 2008 on the popular liberal blog *The Daily Kos*, "our private matter could no longer be wholly private." Not only was Edwards a "dirtbag," he turned everyone around him into one as well.

Now, despite its prominence in the cultural scene, many people other than Elizabeth Edwards claim to want nothing to do with the National Adultery Ritual. These folks frequently insist that our fascination with adultery is a sign of America's lingering Puritanism. Americans, they say, remain neurotic when it comes to matters of sex. They can't accept it as a natural part of the human experience or recognize that sexual behavior has nothing to do with a politician's—or golfer's—competence at his chosen profession. Here's *London Observer*'s Johann Hari in a searing example of the genre after the publication of Elizabeth Edwards's 2009 memoir:

> And so America has finally stumbled on a political issue of real significance. No, not the trifling matters of economic collapse, global warming, or two wars. No—the issue of the day is John Edwards' dick. Since Elizabeth Edwards published a book about the supremely trivial

fact that her husband had an affair, the cable shows have been endlessly debating the "issue" once again.

Memo to America: Grow. Up.

Have you forgotten the lesson of Lewinsky so soon? While al-Qa'ida plotted a murderous attack on the US, the twice-elected president was busy being impeached over a few bouts of consensual oral sex. It meant nothing. It was nothing. But it skewed your politics for years. (*Huffington Post*, May 14, 2009)

Inevitably, Hari goes on to compare America with the "mature model" found in Europe "where politicians' affairs are considered irrelevant," and where no one is interested in their leaders' "meaningless ejaculation[s]. . . . The idea a French president would be debarred from office for sleeping with somebody other than his wife is preposterous."

Hari and his like-minded critics are right about one thing: the National Adultery Ritual is a uniquely American bourgeois exercise. But the origins of our obsession cannot be chalked up to immaturity or sexual hang-ups. No, the ritual is a tribute not to chastity but to fidelity, specifically male fidelity. Hari—a male, in case you hadn't realized—doesn't like it. Many men don't. The truth is the adultery ritual is for women's sake.

Let me explain. For reasons that neurologists and evolutionary psychologists suggest are embedded in the Y chromosome, male promiscuity and infidelity have been a stark fact of human society since, well, since the first man said, "I do." To be sure, women have cheated on their husbands. But throughout time men have always been the less fair sex, as by all surveys, they remain today. Polygamy has been widespread, far more so than monogamy in fact, while polygyny, women with more than one husband, has been exceedingly rare. In ancient Athens married men had their way with female slaves, as did men in the antebellum Confederacy. Extracurricular sex by men was widespread enough to create the market for the world's oldest, and probably most universal, profession. Many cultures have accepted the male predilection for prostitutes as inevitable and even as a safety valve for what Thomas Aquinas called men's "careless lusts." In urban ports all over the world sailors looked for domestic outsourcing for unavailable or reluctant wives. So did men about town like Samuel Pepys or nineteenth-century New York gentlemen where "working women" could be found not just in brothels, but in the many venues where gentlemen hung out—restaurants, clubs, and theaters.

And what did Mrs. Pepys and her wifely comrades make of all of this? Funny, we never heard much about that. The humiliation of cuckolded men launched a thousand Shakespearean jokes, but the two-timed women? In most cultures, the wives of polygamous or cheating men were supposed to accept Big Love without jealousy or complaint, to treat it as so much "meaningless ejaculation." The European approach that Hari approves of is no different really. Mark D. White, a psychologist writing on the *Psychology Today* website, unwittingly evokes the indifference toward wives implicit in the model; "François Mitterrand, who was president of the republic for twelve years toward the end of the twentieth century, had a mistress and a love child whom everybody knew about; in fact they both marched in his funeral procession, behind his official wife. Nobody gave a *merde*. The centrist presidential candidate in the last presidential election openly consorts with his longtime honey, while his Catholic wife stays home with the kids. It's the arrangement they have." It was the arrangement *they* had, see?

What is unusual in the human record is not men stepping out on their wives. What is unusual is the model of faithful monogamy, a model that takes for granted the importance of women's experience, not just men's. Before the eighteenth century and outside of Western Europe, marriage was a social and economic as well as sexual arrangement; it had little to do with love and companionship, and no one much cared about whether women were fulfilled or not. But with the emergence of what sociologists and historians refer to as companionate marriage, intimacy became the marital ideal. Instead of arranged unions, the young made their own choice of mate based on shared interests and deep affection rather than on social requirements. Fidelity followed naturally, or so it was hoped, and it meant that, yes, people gave a *merde*.

Companionate marriage was a remarkable moral advance in social history, particularly for women. The American founders understood this. Rejecting the cynical, paternalistic arrangements of the ancien régime, they saw in the intimate, quasi-egalitarian relations between husbands and wives a reflection of democratic ideals. The model found its perfect expression in the relationship between John and Abigail Adams portrayed in the PBS series a while back. We don't see John cavorting with prostitutes in his many months in Philadelphia away from his wife, his dear friend, though surely his fidelity was something unusual.

To be sure, the model was often little more than a nodding tribute from vice to virtue. Even in the mid-twentieth century, and especially outside the middle class, men strayed and women knew it. JFK's Camelot, for instance, was a land of male sexual privilege, as Jackie Kennedy well understood. So did the reporters and aides who kept her husband's affairs—and those of his brother, FDR, Eisenhower, and Martin Luther King among others—under wraps. It wasn't until 1987, in response to a growing feminist sensibility as well as to an increasing female presence in the press corps, that the media headlined presidential candidate Gary Hart's relationship with a young woman named Donna Rice that adultery became legitimate news. The rest is Clintonian history.

Far from a vestige of American prudery, then, the National Adultery Ritual is best understood as a modern protest on behalf of women against the persistence of male infidelity in an age of equality. In the early 1960s JFK could get away with it; in the 1990s WJC would not. Though he remained in office, Clinton paid a heavy price for his roguish ways. He became the second president in the nation's history to be impeached and stayed stuck in the laughing stocks for years. His chief offense was not oral sex; it was his humiliation of his wife and daughter. People—women especially—cringed at Hillary's embarrassment, as they would at all of what Tina Brown called the "downtrodden political wives called to genuflect before their husbands' outsize egos."

More specifically, the Adultery Ritual is an indictment of male lust for younger women. The "other" woman is almost always dewier, sexier, and a deeply bitter reminder to the middle-aged wife and her peers of their declining allure. No matter how impressive her achievements, depth, or wisdom, the wife is an aging female, the least enviable of human beings. Monica Lewinsky vs. Hillary Clinton. Rielle Hunter vs. Elizabeth Edwards. In a just world, would there be any contest? The bottle-blonde Rielle commenced her seduction by whispering to the candidate, "You're hot"; she passed out business cards inscribed with the words—in caps, of course—"BEING IS FREE. TRUTH SEEKER"; she came on to every man she met; and she appeared in a photo shoot lolling on a bed revealing a naked midsection once full with Edwards child, now bikini-ready. *That's* what men prefer? Then they must be shamed for it.

The ritual's pro-wife rationale is the reason why debate swirls around the question of whether women should appear at press conferences with their husbands. Until recently, they generally did, probably because handlers wanted to dramatize the forgiveness they hoped the public would extend to their bosses. The pathos of Silda Spitzer may have been the final straw. The *Los Angeles Times* ran an article, on the front page no less, disputing the wisdom of Silda's appearance. Is a man's ambition more important than a woman's dignity? the paper wondered. Ridley Scott, the honcho Hollywood producer, even designed a successful, and remarkably nuanced, television series around the dilemma aptly entitled *The Good Wife*. Jenny Sanford, though, may have transformed the ritual forever. Sitting tight with her girlfriends at her beach house, she left her husband to twist in the wind of media attention all by his rambling, lonesome self, and so earned the title "The Savviest Spurned Wife in History" from *Time*. "The cheated-upon spouses of the world have a new hero and her name is Jenny Sanford," announced the magazine in praise of her choice. She has since filed for divorce.

A few male writers have begun to suspect the real meaning of the Adultery Ritual. Mulling over the aftermath of the Spitzer scandal in *New York*, Phillip Weiss waxed sympathetic about "married men tormented by their sexual needs," a compassion he described trying, unsuccessfully, to convince Mrs. Weiss to share. *Vanity Fair* critic Michael Wolff speculated that the country's interest in the topic reflects "revulsion towards middle aged white men. . . . To the degree that, for 50 years, boomers have been expressive about their sexuality, we now have this population of middle-aged showboats helplessly dramatizing theirs." Both men are a lot closer to understanding the moral drama behind the ritual than those who view it as the reproach of busy-body virtuecrats.

So, for all its tawdriness, our adultery obsession has its purpose. Alas, it's unlikely to do much to stem the nation's sorry trends in marriage. As divorce filings from wives—said to outnumber those from husbands—suggest, it's not just men who struggle with long-term monogamy. Nor can infidelity by itself explain the fragile condition of the institution in the United States today. Still, for now and to their credit, Americans continue to believe that there is meaning in those extramarital activities.

2: Monster Mashup
How Our Culture's Heroes and Villains Have Traded Places

Tony Woodlief

I T IS A common scene in old monster movies: the glowing-eyed creature rises from the coffin, or shuffles from the crypt, or creeps from the waters, and his intended victim stands transfixed, her (for it is almost always a woman) face frozen with revulsion and horror, while we in the audience twitch and gesticulate and eventually shout, "Run!"

Which she finally does, too late and badly. Inevitably she's in inappropriate shoes, because in these films when a girl's dog goes missing two things are certain: she will look for him in the foggiest part of town, and she will forget to change into sneakers first. And so she will be drained or devoured, and she will protest, and many of us will wonder why in the world such a sensible-looking girl would put herself in such peril in the first place.

It used to be that "no" really did mean "no," or at least something far more complicated than "yes," but this was before Hawthorne and James and Poe were shunted aside by literati for Freud's hammer of the Id, and suddenly there were nails everywhere. We learned, then, what it *really* means for the prim young girl to be strutting through the dusky swamp in a skirt, and that the gleam in her eye, at the moment of encounter, might be concealing something besides horror. No wonder she didn't run, we discover. The worst caricature of a self-justifying date rapist became, in the hands of Freud-besotted literary theorists, sophisticated criticism.

Most classic monster stories, as Christopher Booker points out in *The Seven Basic Plots*, involve an inhuman, self-satisfying creature that threatens society, and who must in turn be resisted or rooted out and destroyed by members of a community acting in concert. This is true of the monsters Homer sets against Odysseus and his men in the eighth century, and of Bram Stoker's nineteenth-century Dracula, and of the old (1933) and new (2005) King Kong. But what if the pretty young maidens being crushed or devoured or sucked dry have all been protesting a wee bit much? What if, in the words of date rapists and literary theorists, they really "want it"?

The community bent on slaying monsters becomes, then, a cabal of repressive seventeenth-century Puritans. Reading ghosts and fiends as transgressive Others unshackled from traditional sexual mores means the people who want to behead Gorgons and impale bloodsuckers are killjoys or, worse still, hypocrites sublimating their own passions. The Puritans influence American culture far more than we think, and not just in the ways we think, but to most people they are just sexually frustrated witch-burners best characterized by H. L. Mencken as a dour bunch perpetually worried that someone, somewhere, is having a good time.

And monsters, in modern American fiction, are where the fun is. It took them a while, but they finally realized that though a girl may like it rough, she doesn't like it *that* rough, and while they may gently render her inhuman, they ought not to extinguish her life altogether. Thus the renaissance in vampire tales, wherein the bloodsuckers are—hemoglobin being apparently low-carb—svelte and alluring. Some of them remain morally unreconstructed and willing to kill for fun, but at least they go about it with panache. Further, these unrepentant killers are not characteristic of all vampires, they are simply bad seeds. Monsters are no longer, in other words, inherently monstrous.

Thus do some fanged characters in the popular *Twilight* series spare human life, especially when that human life is a creamy young virgin squirming to be deflowered and eventually dehumanized. That's not how *Twilight* devotees would characterize events, of course, because the vampire is no longer a monster. Instead he is like a Canadian exchange student, or someone with an ancient religion to which a girl must convert if she is going to have his pale, toothsome, beautiful babies.

Bram Stoker's Dracula was indisputably a monster. But he has been refashioned, in countless modern tellings and derivatives, as a seducer, a charmer, someone who really knows what the ladies want. He's not the only one to receive such a makeover; though Shakespeare's Romeo is certainly no inhuman monster, he is a self-absorbed narcissist willing to jeopardize community for immediate gratification, and to cowardly kill himself rather than face despair like a man. In modern tellings, though, Romeo is the essence of true love rather than self-love.

And many of us want, it seems, our monsters to be sweeter and sexier. Or maybe we've simply forgotten, living as we do in a prosperous, peaceful society, the creatures born for centuries in the dark recesses of man's imagination, beset as he was by forces beyond his ken or control. In this age when consequences of bad or wicked decisions can be ameliorated, we can afford more tolerance of narcissism, obsession, violence, and recklessness.

And perhaps, myopic as it is, there's merit in beating our sharpened stakes into pegs and welcoming not just God's creatures but the devil's as well into the big tent of cultural acceptance. If even vampires and humans can learn mutual tolerance, if an inhuman Predator can join forces with people to kill even less human Aliens in a 2004 film, and if—lest we forget to pay homage to the predecessors of today's repentant monsters—Darth Vader can rediscover his broken inner child, then who's to say we can't finally broker Middle East peace, or a rapprochement between North and South Korea, or intermarriage between Yankees and Red Sox fans? In an age when we've learned to be more respectful of other species, there's really no reason to go about decapitating or flamethrowing or scorching with sunlight those creatures who simply want to coexist. Especially the good-looking ones.

But alongside this emergence of kinder, gentler monsters is the rise of the monster as hero, and not far behind this the notion that it is men—or, some men, at least—who are the real monsters. And the monsters are the ones who save us from our depraved human selves. The devilish creation Hellboy, for example, in both his 1990s comic book and more recent film incarnations, is prone to fits of temper, but is at root a good guy who protects us from the Nazis. Arnold Schwarzenegger's robot assassin from 1984's *The Terminator*, meanwhile, is humankind's only hope of salvation in the sequel, just as Isaac Asimov's robots were, in his thinking, virtuous mechanical counterparts to Frankenstein's monster. H. G. Wells deployed Martians to beset mankind in *War of the Worlds*, yet the modern movie version dwells not so much on the aliens as on human depravity under duress. Other alien films, meanwhile, treat outer-space visitors as messiahs: E.T., his grown-up brothers in *Close Encounters of the Third Kind*, and their watery cousins in *The Abyss* are all versions of enlightened saviors rescuing people from their own ignorance, other people, or both.

The modern monster is often not only hero and deliverer, but morally superior to the average pilgrim, which is to say all those people who derive no pleasure from comic books and their related films and contemporary Vampire Chic pop lit. Stick the modern protagonist monster in a lineup alongside corporate hacks in suits, and see who today's victims identify as the real threats to humankind. It wasn't the Crow, after all, who oversold us on mortgages and lawn-edging equipment and prescription drugs for the past four decades.

The military-industrial complex behind the rape of a planet in *Avatar*, to take another example, is represented by two of Hollywood's favorite caricatures: the bloodthirsty soldier and the spineless corporate lackey. The two conspire to extract a valuable mineral that resides under the sacred tree of spiritually advanced aliens, and their rapaciousness is only halted once the protagonist joins the aliens not only in spirit but in body, becoming, literally, one of them. While it is intentionally derivative of the 1990 *Dances with Wolves*, among other films, the important difference, which ought to mean something, is that no matter how whites demonized them, the warlike Sioux were human. It was their very humanity, in fact—love for their communities, indignation at having their land stolen, pride and anger and faith and art and all the things that differentiate us from goldfish—that led to their bloody clashes with the U.S. government. Kevin Costner's Lieutenant Dunbar switched sides, but in the bloody tooth-and-claw battle of the species he stayed on the same team. The protagonist in *Avatar*, however, not only betrayed humans and helped another species kill them, he gave up his own humanity.

As in the *Twilight* series, we have stumbled oddly and without irony in a full circle: the monster of old devoured humans, subsuming them into his being; now humans—the enlightened ones, anyway—willingly abandon humanity in favor of assimilation into monsterdom. The Borg and the Bodysnatchers simply needed more attractive spokesmodels, it seems.

And perhaps we can blame, for this topsy-turvy state of affairs, the Puritans themselves. It was they who brought to America's shores, after all, the notion that humankind is inherently wicked, that man is a monster to his core, in fact, unless he happens to be among God's foreordained Elect. Concomitantly it was the Puritans who taught us to be on the lookout to divine, among one another, the signs of election or reprobation. And it was the Puritans who embedded in American culture the notion that physicality is to be distrusted and spirituality exalted. All these beliefs are essential if one is to embrace the notion that literal monsters can be spiritually virtuous and humans thoroughly monstrous.

Can we really fault those in turn who subsequently, viewing God through the Puritan lens, conceptualize him as a monster as well? It's a fairly short path from Calvin's doctrine of Election to the

2010 film *Legion*, wherein the heavenly host, led by the archangel Gabriel, descends from heaven not to establish a kingdom where there are "no more tears nor crying," but to extinguish humankind from the sight of an angry God. And who will save us from this greatest of all monsters?

Why, a fallen angel, of course. Cue the Rolling Stones' "Sympathy for the Devil" as we reread Satan's speech in the early stanzas of *Paradise Lost*. (Not coincidentally is *Legion* set in the fictional town of Paradise Falls.)

To be sure, sometimes the reason for a monster-as-good-guy twist is simply variety—writers can get tired of giving us variations on the same theme. Thus when we anticipate that Shrek's kiss from the princess will transform him into his handsome real self, and instead she becomes a cute little ogre, we are expected to chuckle, and many of us do. She doesn't mind being an ogre, of course, because it's what's underneath that counts. That doesn't seem such a bad message.

One wonders at the source of this creative fatigue, however, given that the monster plot has served well for centuries. Perhaps it is like the Aristotelian tragedy, another durable form that has given way to the all-things-work-together-for-good melodrama, an Americanized perversion of Calvinism, wherein the protagonist always gets the girl, wins the fortune, bests the one-dimensional villains, and thinks up the snappiest one-liner to close the film. Maybe we really have, in other words, approached the creative asymptote.

Or perhaps it's not the limit of creative possibility, writ large, that too many artists have reached, but rather the limits of their own creative abilities. Worse still, perhaps the asymptote against which they are bumping their heads is the expectation of soothing predictability held by the viewing public. Maybe there are no more tragedies because we demand happy endings. Maybe monsters are becoming good guys because we dislike horrible things.

Except that we do like horror—or at least a substantial subset of our youth does, as evidenced by the enduring success of slasher porn like the recent *Hostel* and *Saw* series. It's just that in place of a shark, as in *Jaws*, or demons, as in *The Exorcist* (two of the top-selling horror films of all time), we have *The Texas Chainsaw Massacre, A Clockwork Orange*, and the Hannibal Lecter films. Our monsters are no longer different species, they are depraved human beings.

Perhaps this isn't surprising, given the mass violence unleashed by human on human in the twentieth century. Every century has known its killers and conquerors, of course, but only in modern times has killing been both mass-produced and depersonalized. We have banished the darkness to the edges of our suburbs, but there is no remedying, it seems, the darkness in our hearts. Maybe the emergence of man as monster is simply a reflection of this reality, or a recognition of it.

Except that we are still left with the troubling corollary played out in so much modern fiction: not only are men now monsters, but monsters are increasingly the equivalent of what, in earlier fiction, were virtuous men. If Descartes and Freud were right, and the mind is both proof and prison, then the most creative and diabolical monster available to a writer is the self-originating beast called man. Yet we cannot help but yearn for virtue, for heroes, and in a world where God is an abstraction or an absence or an enemy whose finest creation is monstrous, the role of savior falls to monsters. Milton's Satan seems to approvingly anticipate: "The mind is its own place and in itself / Can make a Heaven of Hell, a Hell of Heaven."

"Not everybody can play the hero," a young man is told near the beginning of *Legion*. Except that he does become the hero at the end, by virtue of receiving ill-defined but significant powers from the fallen angel. Physically changed to look like what by definition is a demon, he is renamed a "true protector." He and his new gal drive off into the sunset, armed to the teeth lest they need to defend themselves further against the minions of a murderous God.

Does it matter, this inversion of devils and men, of demons and angels? Perhaps only as much as any wave in culture's sea. Film and fiction don't shape culture so much as reflect it, yet in doing so they certainly afford some measure of reinforcement. They tell us what we do, and in turn, should think about the question: what is the nature of man?

The early church certainly had an answer, that man is created in the image and likeness of God. Calvin and his Puritan descendants didn't disagree, but they embraced the additional doctrine that man is thoroughly corrupted because of Adam and Eve's indiscretion in the Garden. When theologians tell us man is profane, and philosophers declare him simply matter or will or ego, then little wonder that writers make him a monster, and seek out, in creatures humanlike but uncorrupted by humanity, a better race of being. "Art has become so dreadful," writes theologian Edward T. Oakes, "precisely because contemporary man denies that he has been made in the image of Christ."

It's an intriguing idea, that the root of this problem lies not in the soul of a Spielberg or Tarantino or Cameron, but in the worldview of many good church people who like to denounce them. But to be fair to good church people, perhaps they are simply speaking the truth about man, who certainly doesn't have a track record of distinction when it comes to decent living. And so perhaps we get the art we deserve, as Milton's archangel Michael might agree, declaring that man is "defaced . . . worthily since they / God's image did not reverence in themselves."

3: Chick Lit and the Master/Slave Dialectic

Meghan Cox Gurdon

T HE ANCIENT ROMANS had an annual holiday of which they were very fond. Saturnalia, which came in December roughly around the time we celebrate Christmas and Hanukkah, was a time of revelry, gambling, and festive dress during which, daringly, masters and slaves played at switching roles. The game had limits: masters might indeed serve lavish suppers to their slaves, but it was still the slaves who did the cooking, such as stuffing and roasting the dormice that were a delicacy of the era.

We can't go back into the minds of the Romans, but the popularity of the holiday and the jovial way in which the ancients referred to it ("loose reins are given to public dissipation," wrote Seneca) suggest that Saturnalia may have worked as a kind of safety valve: a bit of risky glee that once a year eased the burden of a slave's enslavement while reminding his master that mastery was as much an accident of fate as anything else.

The German thinker Georg Hegel thought a great deal about questions of Master and Slave, but he took a dim view of festivals such as Saturnalia and was not a fan of Rome (he preferred the Greeks). In his *Philosophy of History*, Hegel writes about the "scurrilous dances and songs" that attended Roman festivities. Transmitted through the page, we can almost see his lip curling in disdain when he observes that ancient holidays such as Saturnalia produced vulgar merriment that "degenerated into buffoonery unrelieved by intellect."

It's a good thing Hegel didn't live long enough to discover "chick lit," one of our own culture's valves for letting off suppressed social steam. I doubt he would have liked it. He would probably have dismissed out of hand this frothy, female-centered literary type, produced chiefly by British and American authors, not least for the genre's tendency toward bright pink, orange, and red dust-jackets and its encouragement of hysteria.

Yet Hegel would have easily spotted within the pages of chick lit one of his own best-remembered ideas: the theory of the Master/Slave dialectic. In Hegel's explanatory myth, tension arises when two self-conscious beings encounter one another somewhere in the ether. Each takes the other to be a mere object, and the two begin a struggle so terrible it seems destined to end only in one party's death. The battle ends instead in the emergence of the Master and the subjugation of the Slave.

Even after winning, though, the Master isn't content, because the Slave can't be completely controlled. The Slave, unsurprisingly, manifests dissatisfaction by continuing to rebel.

Ultimately, the combatants are made to see that only in recognizing each other's humanity can each accept the other's existence and cease the perilous conflict. Harmony ensues, at which point the Park Avenue hostess runs off with the hunky Manny and the haggard, high-heeled, Type-A barrister quits her practice to start an organic salad company and spend more time with her children.

Oh, wait! Forgive me; that was the chick lit talking. Hegel may have conceived of these tensions being worked out by bloodless archetypes on an esoteric plane, but they crop up everywhere in the pages of light novels. The extremes of Master and Slave are greatly attenuated, of course; you won't find a Simon Legree in these stories. Indeed, as we shall see, the master is in many cases not an actual person—a housewife or a nanny or a backstabbing boss—but an oppressive idea. Yet the wrangle between domi-nance and submission recurs almost endlessly, and the outcomes have surprising Hegelian similarities.

We meet a high-powered attorney who was demoted overnight and is working as a housekeeper, a submissive Indian village girl suddenly transported to glittering L.A. hierarchies, a suburban housewife tempted by single-gal gaiety, chic singletons hungering for domesticity, and countless antic she-lawyers who are desper-ately trying to juggle their nannies, jobs, children, and tousled-architect husbands—in that order.

Wherever settings they portray, chick lit novels allow us vicari-ously to experience the stressful argy-bargy of the modern female experience. And like little hardback Saturnalias, they serve to vent the steam that builds up for women who are almost boiling from the pressure of trying to "have it all."

For, as everyone knows, early twenty-first-century woman is conflicted. She wants to be liberated and independent and pro-fessionally successful, but she also wants to keep a man. She loves her children (if she has them, and if she doesn't have them, she secretly wants them), yet they cut into time she'd rather spend doing other things and she's guilt-ridden about it. She's frazzled from juggling all things, not to mention bone-tired, yet she obeys the imperative to remain toned and sexy.

Most important, the demanding nature of her life requires that she suppress the unpleasant reality that, as a husband in one novel tells his workaholic wife, "We need you and you need to enjoy life again and get off this treadmill. You're like a hamster, running, running . . ."

Kate Reddy is surely the best-known harassed working mother in contemporary fiction. In Allison Pearson's *I Don't Know How She Does It* (2002), we meet the talented hedge-fund manager and mother of two late one night in her chaotic London kitchen. She's deliberately mangling store-bought mince pies so that she can pass them off later as homemade at her daughter's school

Christmas party. Finally, dropping with fatigue, she goes upstairs but not to bed—yet:

> I take my time brushing my teeth. A count of twenty for each molar. If I stay in the bathroom long enough, Richard will fall asleep and will not try to have sex with me. If we don't have sex, I can skip a shower in the morning. If I skip the shower, I will have time to start on the e-mails that have built up while I've been away and maybe even get some presents bought on the way to work. Only ten shopping days until Christmas, and I am in possession of precisely nine gifts, which leaves twelve to get plus stocking fillers for the children. And still no delivery from KwikToy, the rapid on-line present service.
>
> "Kate, are you coming to bed?" Rich calls from the bedroom.
>
> His voice sounds slurry with sleep. Good.

Kate is running, running. . . . She spends as much time dodging her husband and children as she does talking to them; she resents her nanny but lavishes the woman with gifts for fear she'll quit, and at work she's constantly behind and having to cover for it.

In Sophie Kinsella's *The Undomestic Goddess* (2005), meanwhile, Samantha Sweeting has been running so hard and so long that she can't remember the last time she took a weekend off. A single twenty-nine-year-old with a wardrobe of sleek Armani suits, Samantha is on the fast track to make partner at her prestigious London firm when she makes a catastrophic legal error.

Half mad with distress, she takes a train out of the city, arrives in a quaint village, and, suffering from a horrific headache, stops at a grand house to ask whether there's a hotel nearby. The owners, Trish and Eddie, offer her water and an aspirin and seem curiously eager to explain how they like their furniture dusted.

I manage a half smile.

"You've been very kind, letting me trespass on your evening."

"Her English is good, isn't it?" Eddie raises his eyebrows at Trish.

"She's English!" says Trish triumphantly, as though she's pulled a rabbit out of a hat. "Understands everything I say!"

I am really not getting something here. Do I look foreign?

There's been a comical misunderstanding: Trish and Eddie think Samantha is applying for a job as their housekeeper. Such is our heroine's dizziness at her predicament—the legal fiasco, the terror that she won't make partner—that somehow she doesn't quite get around to declining the couple's job offer. Samantha soon discovers that her smooth capabilities in law do not translate into competence at more traditional woman's work.

By three o'clock I am utterly knackered. I'm only halfway down my list and I can't see myself ever making it to the end. I don't know how people clean houses. It's the hardest job I've ever done, ever.

I am not moving smoothly from task to task like Mary Poppins. I'm darting from unfinished job to unfinished job like a headless chicken.

Yet the longer Samantha stays in her menial role, the more she begins to enjoy it. Fierce ambition has hitherto blinded her to the quieter pleasures of life: sitting down to eat breakfast, for instance, or making bread, or rolling around in the shrubbery with a handsome, educated, yet conveniently easy-going gardener.

Samantha is eventually redeemed professionally (the legal

mistake wasn't hers), but she shocks society, and herself, by fore-going the glittering promises of worldly success for a life spent polishing silver, scrubbing lavatories, and taking a pint at the pub in the evenings. A permanent Saturnalia.

Hegel called this moment *Aufhebung*, when conflicting things are brought together and raised to a higher level. In chick lit, we call this "the ending," in which struggle culminates with the satisfaction of female self-actualization.

But wait, you ask, who's the Master in these scenarios anyway? Is it Samantha Sweeting's employers? Or a diabolical boss, as in Lauren Weisberger's *The Devil Wears Prada* (2003)? Is it a brutally demanding mother-in-law, as in Kavita Daswani's *The Village Bride of Beverly Hills* (2004)? Or perhaps it might be the enthusiastic yet sinister nanny in Suzanne Berne's *A Perfect Arrangement* (2001)?

It is none of these, for the Master isn't a person at all. It's an idea: it is the ambitious, fast-paced, affluent lifestyle (with or without children) to which the heroine has dedicated herself in the belief that it will bring her satisfaction and acclaim.

Only when things get extremely sticky do our ladies realize that in order to be happy they must actually repudiate what they believed would ensure them a fabulous life. This being a post-feminist era, generally they're not abandoning their husbands or children to seek liberation. At the moment of crisis, however, they realize that they must reject their own enslavement by a culture that too greatly prizes wealth and professional achievement.

Amber Winslow has this Aha! moment in Jane Green's *Swapping Lives* (2005), after she trades her lacquered life as a charity hostess in a Connecticut suburb for a month with that of Vicky Townsley, an unmarried London magazine editor. At first Amber finds the experience exhilarating, though soon she begins to miss her husband and children. Oddly, though, she feels no longing for her normal deluxe surroundings. It's only when she visits the loving, messy home of Vicky's brother and sister-in-law in the English countryside that Amber suddenly achieves her *Aufhebung*:

> "That's it!" Amber says suddenly. "That's how I feel! Kate, you've just put your finger on it!"
>
> "What do you mean?"
>
> "I mean that I'm not in control of my life. I have a full-time nanny, a cleaning team that comes three times a week to thoroughly clean my house, a gardening team, a swimming pool man. Other people decorate my house, the nanny does the cooking. Oh my gosh," and she goes quiet as she thinks about the reality of her life. "I'm living my life but I'm not involved in it. That's exactly what's wrong with me."
>
> "But if you're not involved in it, how are you really living it?" Kate asks gently.
>
> "That's the point." Amber shakes her head, the weight of the realization sitting firmly on her shoulders. "I'm not living. I'm just existing, I guess, as though I'm caught in limbo, watching my life play out in front of me like a movie! Oh my God, do you have any idea how huge this is?"

Amber returns to America, where she and her husband quit the rat race and exchange their mansion for an apple orchard in upstate New York where they will rusticate in "an eighteenth-century farmhouse, picture perfect, surrounded by a picket fence with clouds of lavender and catmint, the farm shop across the road next to the orchards, a playground, and a barnyard complete with chickens, geese, sheep, goats, three (little) pigs, two cows, and a pony."

Take that, Type-A lifestyle! Amber's revelations are helped to their satisfactory conclusion by the discovery that her patrician husband, whom she has believed to be a reigning Master of the Universe, has been secretly unemployed. Rather than taking the train to Manhattan to work, for six months Richard's been killing time at the local aquarium.

For the husband not to be as rich as he seems turns out to be a common device. In Emma McLaughlin and Nicola Kraus's *Nanny Returns* (2009), the sequel to *The Nanny Diaries* (2002), the philandering, work-obsessed father known as Mr. X turns out to have been paying for his family's stinking richness with the proceeds of a Ponzi scheme.

In Holly Peterson's *The Manny* (2007), ace network-news producer and mother of three Jamie Whitfield too finds out that her millionaire husband is a crook. In her case, however, she uses the information to blackmail Phillip into letting her leave their diamond-encrusted mode of life.

> "Phillip, I don't want to live in the cloistered environment of Park Avenue with all those provincial wealthy families anymore. And I don't want our children there either."
> "If you're going to knock the way I—"
> "This is not directed at you. In fact, it's not about you. It's about me. And my happiness, and the ultimate well-being of our children. I want to live in a different community. A less judgmental community."

Jamie doesn't want Phillip to join her in Tribeca or Park Slope or wherever she decides, though. She wants Peter Bailey, the male nanny she'd hired to exude manliness around the house while her husband was out harvesting big Gs. She had first glimpsed Peter in Central Park—"I couldn't help but notice how his worn-out khakis traced the lines of his impossibly hard ass"—and swiftly hired him to look after her children. With Peter's help, Jamie comes to see the shallowness and grotesquerie of Park Avenue. The story ends with Jamie, like all heroines in chick lit beach-reads, getting not only what she wants, but also validation:

> Peter pulled me over to the wall away from the passengers and the commotion [at the airport]. "You are so damn beautiful. You are so strong and resilient. You are the most unbelievably sexual and sensual being I have ever been with. All the stumbling blocks that have fallen in your path in the past year will crumble beneath you; you're almost over them already. You are so much more together than when I first met you: so much smarter, so much more aware."

Jamie is unusual in the genre for choosing to smash up her nuclear family (and "do the Manny") to achieve her *Aufhebung*. Much more frequently, as with Amber the life-swapper and Amanda Bright in Danielle Crittenden's *amandabright@home* (2003), the Hegelian struggle results in the heroine renouncing almost everything else in order to rededicate herself to the people who love her most. For Amanda, revelation of what actually matters in life arrives along with her third child, when she nearly dies in the last minutes of labor before the baby is born:

> There is this moment, there is this person, there is this love, there is this life. That's all there is, and it is . . . enough.

Kate Reddy, meanwhile, who's been running and running and running, only comes to a stop when her nanny tells her over a transatlantic phone line that her husband, Richard, has left her. Stunned, Kate asks the nanny to read the letter he'd left for her.

I try to think of the last time I saw him. Saw him properly, I mean, not just the way you see a blur in the rearview mirror. In the past few months, I go out and he takes over or he leaves and I take over. We swap instructions in the hall. We say Emily has eaten a good lunch, so don't worry too much about her tea. We say Ben needs an early night because he wouldn't take a nap this afternoon. We say bowel movements have been successful or are still pending and perhaps some prunes would help. Or else we leave notes. Sometimes we barely meet each other's eyes. Kate and Richard, like a relay team where each runner suspects the other of being the weaker link, but the main thing is to keep running round the track so the baton can be exchanged and the race can go on and on.

The race can't go on. Kate comes to see that her entire family's happiness depends on her making drastic changes. In a turn of plot that will, at this point, not be surprising, Kate quits her big-city job. She and Richard trade their London house, move to the country, and buy "a place on the edge of a market town with a view and a paddock." Kate takes her children to the park, is happily "bored to the point of manslaughter," and is ultimately asked to help finance a faltering factory that makes pretty dollhouses and employs mostly women. Balance achieved! Hurrah!

Taken together, the body of chick lit—of which we have here enjoyed but a taste—gives curious insights to our time and place. "Buffoonery unrelieved by intellect," the genre may be, but it tells us something about who we are.

We can look through these pages, as if through windows, into other people's houses. We can study fictional families that may be outlandish for narrative purposes, yet which also in some important ways may well reflect our own. In the early twenty-first century, there's widespread preoccupation with ambition and success. There's also, for millions of women, a haunting dread that worldly success can exact domestic costs that are painful to contemplate. Never in history have as many people been as rich or had as much abundance of choice than in our era—even (so far) after the successive financial crises that have rocked the confidence of the West. No wonder women are conflicted, and not surprising, then, that so many seek relief in the black-and-white pages of pink-jacketed Saturnalias.

4: Lonely Hearts Online

Why I'm Glad I Didn't Meet My Husband on Match.com

Megan Basham

"How did you two meet?" It may be the most frequent question any couple can expect to hear over the course of their marriage. They'll be asked as newlyweds, they'll be asked as parents mixing with other soccer moms and NASCAR dads, and if the union lasts long enough, they'll certainly be asked at their golden anniversary.

Though we are only in our thirties, the answer my husband and I have for that enduring social inquiry is fast becoming a relic: we met at church. Couples whose responses include work, school, coffee shops, or nightclubs can also count themselves dinosaurs in this brave new wired world. With the exception of being introduced by friends, the most popular way for singles to meet today is online.

According to a 2010 nationally representative survey out of Stanford University, one in four people who started a serious relationship in the last two years met their mate on the Internet. That's a pretty staggering number, especially considering it only counts those that found love on the Web, not the millions more who are trying to. Other studies show that as many as 46 percent of all American singles now avail themselves of dedicated dating sites, using everything from general services like eHarmony and Match.com to specialty matchmakers like JDate.com for Jewish singles or EbonyFriends.com for African Americans.

While the dating sites with their detailed questionnaires and "scientific" matching systems tend to skew older—most of their members are thirty and older—Facebook and MySpace are taking their turn playing Cupid with the next generation. Researchers haven't yet compiled much in the way of hard data on couples meeting on community sites, but popular Facebook dating applications like Zoosk and articles in men's magazines offering tips for picking up girls via social networking suggest it's happening. Microsoft is even advertising its new KIN group of phones by stressing their potential for forming Facebook romances.

On the face of it, there's no reason the Internet shouldn't revolutionize the way we date. After all, it's revolutionized all other forms of personal communication. But its sheer voraciousness with regard to romantic relationships makes it troubling. A huge proportion of people now look to the Web as their primary dating venue, yet the way we forge friendships hasn't undergone a similarly radical change. There are no companies making hundreds of millions of dollars helping people make new pals, and the third of American adults on MySpace and Facebook typically use the sites to find and keep up with old ones. We still form platonic relationships the old-fashioned way—meeting through common interests, backgrounds, or professions. The unique nature of online love and the rate at which it is swallowing up other, more tried-and-true methods of meeting begs certain questions, namely, what is the quality of the relationships being forged online and what are the long-term implications for the way we find love?

In 2002 *Wired* magazine predicted, "Twenty years from now, the idea that someone looking for love without looking for it online will be silly, akin to skipping the card catalog to instead wander the stacks because 'the right books are found only by accident.'" Perhaps they should have been more confident in their forecasting ability and cut their time frame in half.

Online romance has undergone a radical image overhaul in the last ten years from something seen as a last refuge for the housebound, unattractive, or socially inept to the fastest-growing method for finding a mate. To quote that eighties teen classic, *Can't Buy Me Love*, it's gone from geek to chic. Yet data on how these couples' relationships stack up against those who met via more traditional methods is hard to locate. No reliable divorce statistics for Web-launched couples exist, nor have many surveys been published measuring the level of satisfaction these spouses have with their relationships. The only thing we can be sure of is that a great many trips down the aisle these days started with a click of the mouse, which leads me to wonder—if all the numbers are so good, why is the anecdotal evidence so poor?

Maybe it's just that my circle of friends, coworkers, and acquaintances haven't gotten the hang of high-tech hookups, but out of the many, many people I know who have dated someone they met over the Internet, only one or two have had good experiences. Most of the rest are bad. Not merely the we-met-for-coffee-didn't-really-hit-it-off-and-that-was-that kind of bad, but rather the we-met-and-got-married-three-months-later-and-after-one-or-two-excruciating-years-together-divorced-leaving-our-lives-in-a-shambles kind of bad.

One example: while I was working on this essay an old friend came to visit whose marriage had recently broken up. A tall, thirty-something professional in admirable physical shape, he described meeting his ex-wife on Chemistry.com (he had also dated several women through eHarmony). Before six months were out, they married. Before the year was out, they divorced. He said he knew his relationship was in trouble when she refused his friend request on Facebook.

As our friend described the misery of discovering that the woman he had such chemistry with was not the family-oriented single mom he thought her but instead a party girl who often left her five-year-old daughter in his care to hit the club scene, he added, "But I know marriage is hard for everybody." My husband and I exchanged glances, wordlessly sharing the sentiment, "Sure, sometimes it's hard, but it's not *that* hard."

A soldier of our acquaintance also had a less-than-storybook ending to his online romance. He and his wife met on eHarmony. While he was deployed she met another man on MySpace, and he came home to an empty house. Their divorce finalized, he's on the market again, once more looking to the Internet to guide him to his soulmate. Another Internet-formed couple in our circle has made it through four years and two children, but all the indicators at dinner parties and in private conversations with either the husband or wife suggest the marriage is rocky.

Of course I'm not so foolish as to assume that the few negative instances I've witnessed necessarily represent the whole online dating scene, but even some of those involved in creating that scene admit their methods may not be as effective as more old-school approaches. Relationship psychologist James Houran, who developed algorithms for the dating site PlentyofFish.com, recently told ABC News that whatever compatible characteristics two individuals may share, he guesses relationships created online are more likely to fail than those launched the old-fashioned way.

Companies like Chemistry.com, Perfectmatch.com, and eHarmony have done a brilliant job selling "scientific" compatibility. In 2005 a study by the Pew Internet and American Life Project found that 64 percent of single Internet users agree that online dating helps people find a better match than they would on their own. Only 28 percent disagree. Any other industry would be thrilled to have a customer base so confident in its product. Yet at this stage the success they point to is almost solely measured by quantity not quality. eHarmony claims responsibility for "two percent of all new marriages." Match.com crows that twelve of their members get married or engaged every day. Even if these numbers are accurate (never mind that the *Wall Street Journal* did an excellent investigative piece demonstrating that they're probably not), what do they prove?

It's not surprising that a lot of people who make use of online dating sites end up wedded. If people are willing to spend the money and time answering surveys and corresponding with matches, one has to suppose that most of them want to get married. So it should come as no surprise that a 2010 study conducted by sociologists at Iowa State University found that online couples go from meeting to matrimony in less than half the time of those who meet through more low-tech methods.

Those few researchers who are in the early stages of studying couples created by dating sites (those who aren't employed by the very same sites, that is) say they have yet to note any appreciable benefit of the service. Jeffrey Lohr, a professor of psychology at the University of Arkansas who is studying the claims of these companies, says that they are "marketing their product far beyond the available evidence. There is none to very little effectiveness in the matching process."

Regardless of the Web's spotty track record for fostering love connections, with so much of our lives lived online it is extremely unlikely the tide of Internet dating is going to turn back now. Professional dating sites may gain or lose credibility as more research comes out, but people who already use the Internet to go to school, find jobs, and maintain friendships are still going to use it for life's most tender pursuit. And even those relationships founded on face-to-face first meetings will increasingly feel the impact of the wired culture for good or for ill.

Taking the love doctors and their dating sites out of the discussion, the idea that the Internet makes better matches than real-world interaction remains pervasive. In particular, many enthusiasts posit that social-networking sites such as Facebook and MySpace give people with similar interests and life priorities a chance to recognize themselves in another's profile.

This reference will date me, but hearing singles extol the superiority of trolling for dates on Facebook because it allows them to pinpoint people who like the same music, movies, or leisure activities they do reminds me of an episode from the long-running NBC sitcom *Friends* where the friends get into a contest over who knows each other better. One of the *Jeopardy*-style questions put to the guys is, "Rachel claims this is her favorite movie . . ." Answer: *Dangerous Liaisons*. The follow-up question provides the zinger: "But her actual favorite movie is . . ." *Weekend at Bernie's*. All three guys get the right answer because they've spent enough time hanging around Rachel that they can see past the person she thinks she is to the person they know her to be. If Ross had met Rachel on MySpace, he'd probably think *Dangerous Liaisons* was her favorite film to this day.

By the same token, when faith-minded friends tell me that they like dating and social-networking sites because they can sift through the secular chaff and find the religious wheat quickly (because what could be a stronger spiritual proclamation than checking "Christian" in the Facebook religion box?), I think, doesn't church already do a better and certainly more reliable job of that?

A man may write in a profile or answer in a questionnaire that faith is important to him because he thinks it *should* be important to him. It doesn't necessarily mean that he darkens the doorstep of a church any days other than Christmas and Easter. Or, frankly, it could simply mean that he thinks churchgoing girls are more likely to be nice-looking and respectable—the kind of girls he can settle down and start a family with.

The idea that what people write on their Facebook profiles or answer in personality questionnaires is a perfect reflection of who they actually are is demonstrably naive. It can just as easily reflect who they want to be or whom they want others to think they are more than it does the true person. That goes doubly for the young.

If I'd had a Facebook page in my late teens and early twenties, I probably would have posted pictures and links that made me look flirtatious, impulsive, and carefree because at the time it's who I aspired to be. Thank God when I met my husband I either did such a miserable job aping these qualities that he never thought I had them or he saw through my performance to the bookish, contemplative, compulsive planner who was perfect for him.

Not that people can't lie about both trivialities and important values in person, but the spontaneity of in-person socializing makes it less likely they will do so, or at least do so successfully. The very nature of the profile page allows people infinite time to shape an idealized persona. Case in point: as I write this, an article posted on the popular men's site AskMen.com offers to educate men on how to craft a Facebook page that will attract women.

If you're curious about their advice, they suggest staying away from spontaneous postings of videos, games, or jokes that dudes like but women might find geeky or crude. Similarly, guys should avoid revealing anything that could "become a deal breaker for a woman . . . such as not wanting kids or not believing in marriage," and they should absolutely delete those comments from buddies that smack of wild partying, which may be off-putting to the ladies. As for what *should* go on single men's profiles, Ask-Men recommends photos that make them look well traveled and regular status updates that smack of mystery like "heading downtown."

It may all sound a little calculated (and corny) for an application that was designed to let people find old friends and update their social circle about their daily activities, but they make some fair, if fairly creepy, points. As big as the Internet's potential for bringing couples together is, it's nothing compared to its enormous capacity for keeping good mates apart.

Something about that blank profile page or open Twitter box prompts our most exhibitionist tendencies. During our regular brick-and-mortar activities we wouldn't presume to share intimate details about our sex lives with casual acquaintances or bore them with every quasi-mystical thought that flits through our brains. (The phrase "Facebook-dumped" entered the lexicon after so many people found out their romances were over not in face-to-face conversation but after reading it on the site's news feed.) Yet every stripe of self-important, inappropriate, and occasionally brutal preening is deemed okay for the Internet. On the one hand, we use these applications because we assume people are watching; on the other we often seem not to realize . . . *people are watching!*

Those who prefer Web-based introductions because they think it gives them more control over how they present themselves might want to consider what a diligent Google sleuth can turn up. Where you live, the value of the house you own, how you looked on a particularly bad hair day are just the beginning. Enter all the commentary littering a profile page into the equation, and two people who might have felt sparks fly in person reject each other out of hand.

As one dating coach who advises against Internet romance told the *Washington Post*, "We make determinations about somebody, whereas if we met them and we liked them, it wouldn't be as big a deal." She cites politics in particular, with clients telling her that they declined a meeting after some Web snooping revealed that a potential date contributed money to a candidate or supported a cause they didn't like (good thing Mary Matalin and James Carville didn't try to find spouses this way).

If the Internet really was just one more way to navigate the sea of people looking for love, the possibility of misjudging a person who could be a great fit wouldn't be such a hazard. However, when it takes so much precedence over older, more road-tested methods of finding a soulmate it becomes worrisome. Is it possible that it is the effortless, nonthreatening nature of Internet dating and not its superiority that leads people to prefer it to tried-and-true options?

"Busy-ness" is the number one reason single people give for dating online. But are we really that much busier than we were in the 1990s or 1980s? Or is it simply less scary to log onto a website and start corresponding with matches than to attend a flesh-and-blood event where one must reach out a hand and introduce oneself to a stranger? Do singles really spend less time trolling on Facebook than they would getting involved in some kind of organization where they are more assured of meeting like-minded people?

Reward is almost always achieved in proportion to the risk and time involved. Trying to get to know people, face-to-face, at a place of worship, a charity event, or another social gathering feels infinitely more risky than posting a comment online, at home, alone. Realizing, over time, that you might want to share more than a laugh at the coffeepot with the guy in the next cubicle is a slow process, but a profound one. By contrast, the narrow aim and impatient spirit of online dating—*I am here to fall in love and I want to do it now*—seems antithetical to the very idea of romance.

5: In My Humble Opinion
Why Americans Still Need Advice Columnists

Margo Howard

SOMEONE ONCE ASKED Dan Savage, the syndicated relationship-advice columnist, what qualifies him to give advice. "Because someone asks," he answered smartly.

Still, it's a good question.

Most advice columnists, like my mother, the late Ann Landers, do not have special degrees in psychology or counseling. They can hardly speak to every situation from experience either. In fact, it definitely takes chutzpah with a capital CH to give advice to strangers day in and day out.

But it is at the same time a humbling endeavor. Trying to find "the right answer" with not a lot of information—and only one side of the story—is certainly a leap of faith. As everyone knows, it is easier to see a problem from the outside.

I have received letters from women in verbally abusive relationships. They want to know whether to get a divorce. Or whether that would be worse for the kids. There are times I have advised divorce.

But what if the results are disastrous? I will bear responsibility for making someone's life worse, not better.

During my mother's tenure—forty-seven years—one of her trademarks was going to experts in whatever field was being discussed if she did not have the information or instinct to craft an answer. She was famous for hitting up the top authorities in many disciplines and passing on their answers. She used to say in her speeches, "My advice may be free to you, but you should see my phone bills."

Some advice columns go heavy on recommending service agencies and resources for all manner of problems. My mother actually started this. At the time when what is now Health and Human Services was known as HEW (Health, Education, and Welfare), Joe Califano, then the agency head, would often have someone call Mother's office for information because her files of city agencies and free services in every town that carried her column were more complete than theirs. (The reason for this was that Ann Landers was the most widely syndicated text column in the world, with 1,250 newspapers. And because she viewed her mission as one of service, her staff made it their business to research agencies in every town and city carrying her column, just as they responded to every letter that came with a name and address.)

Living in the age of the Internet, as we do now, there is a boatload of online resources, and most people know how to find them. In fact, they can be rather overwhelming at a certain point. It is for that reason that my modus operandi is to have my column's answers come from my gut. This is one of the few careers I can think of where a practitioner can succeed, at many levels, without "training," because useful advice comes from maturity, experience, education, judgment, and common sense . . . which ain't so common.

Every advice columnist who is at all serious about the work has to come to it with humility, as well as trusting one's own philosophy. It is no small thing to write what is read by millions of people—with at least some percentage of them taking your word as gospel.

A proverb listed in many collections, including *Poor Richard's Almanack*, strikes me as germane to the advice column: "He that will not be counseled cannot be helped." Asking for guidance, even from a person unknown to you, is a beginning, a way to start straightening up some of the messes of life. The funny thing about reading an advice column is that the stranger with the byline comes to feel like a friend.

There are numerous reasons people will write to a stranger asking for help. One is anonymity. I remember that my mother periodically got this explanation from a correspondent: "I cannot go to my clergyman because I am my clergyman." I now receive letters from people in small towns who feel unable to visit a mental health professional because they know them socially. Or they have no insurance. Or they simply don't know where help is available. I think the saddest reason for writing to an advice column is that the troubled person literally has no one else to talk to. A great many people are alone in the world, which for some of us is almost unimaginable.

An interesting thing that perhaps only an advice columnist would know is that there is a subtle embarrassment about needing to write to a stranger. So many letters begin: "I never thought in a million years I would be writing to you . . ." or "This is the first time I have written to an advice column." Getting over that hump can be a humbling experience.

Another thing I never knew until I started this work was that often people will ask for advice because they're looking for affirmation. I cannot count the number of people who e-mail me back (I do not deal with snail mail, as my mother did, and some others still do) saying, essentially, "I knew I should do what you suggested, but I just needed to hear it from someone else." As Erica Jong put it, "Advice is what we ask for when we already know the answer but wish we didn't." So one important function of the advice column is that it becomes the voice that says out loud what the writer may, in fact, be thinking. The affirmation of the outsider is surprisingly persuasive, and the longer you ply the trade, if you build up credibility, your word begins to carry authority, which then morphs into trust. And let us not forget in these times of financial hardship and insurance confusion, the advice column is free.

A common misperception (by those who are untroubled, I might add) is that "only the goofs write in," as some people used to imprudently suggest to my mother. To cite Bill Cosby, he with a doctorate in education no less, "A word to the wise ain't necessary, it's the stupid ones who need the advice." I could not disagree more. I get mail from the highly educated, name partners in law firms, senior clergymen, lawyers, doctors, those with .gov addresses, and senior management. And all with problems. Trouble is no respecter of position, and certainly not education.

I hope I've addressed the question of why people write to advice columns. Now let's talk about why people read them. Do they just get a kick out of watching the foibles of others?

Voyeurism is certainly high on the list, but I would say not in the pejorative sense of the word. Let us call it eavesdropping, in spirit, on other people's problems. The effect of this can be manifold— and here's where virtue comes in. The advice column as an educational tool should not be underestimated. For whatever reason, people who read advice columns tend to read them religiously, and they often follow more than one. General information can be gleaned, which often proves useful at some time in the future. When faced with a particular situation, someone else's letter may come to mind. The advice column reader—consciously or not— already has a possible approach in mind. In an ongoing discussion with readers, both a belief system and a set of values are imparted. (The columnist's.) People pick up on this, even if reflexively. I've been quite surprised by the number of readers who have let me know that their game was to imagine how they would respond to a problem before reading my answer.

For the close reader, an advice column becomes a form of ongoing education about human behavior. There are just so many problems, after all, as I have learned in twelve years of dealing with them. Because of the faithful readership respected advice columns can enjoy, the public good can be advanced. An example: during the Nixon presidency my mother asked her readers to write their representatives in Washington to lobby for a huge increase in federal funding for cancer research. (She both understood her power and had an exceptionally loyal audience.) Well, one million pieces of mail flooded Capitol Hill—more letters than were received about the Vietnam War—and Nixon wound up signing a $100 million bill aimed at cancer research, the first massive federal grant addressed to combating a specific disease.

For many, the advice column is a real-life soap opera that one reads instead of watches. There are two general categories of response: either schadenfreude or gratitude that there but for the grace of God . . .

It is beneficial to have reminders that others have it worse than you. Being privy to other people's problems is one way to achieve perspective on some of life's annoyances . . . so that even if the advice column is read as entertainment, the by-product can be inspiring, elevating, or educational.

6: All the President's Friends
The Challenge of Loyalty in Politics

Pia Catton

BETRAYALS AND BACKSTABBINGS are the natural, renewable resources of Hollywood. What's a gossip magazine without a jagged hot-pink line drawn between photos of two suddenly former BFF starlets?

It's a little too easy, however, to criticize Los Angeles as a place where loyalty runs only as deep as a Botox needle. To be sure, it is an image-obsessed town where friendships are essentially disposable: there's no point spending time with someone who might jeopardize your ascent to fame, fortune, and a permanent spot on the A-list. This makes it very much like Washington, DC—although there the game is even more complicated.

One would expect political loyalties to have a certain intellectual basis. After all, the common ground among like-minded players is ideology, issues, and elections—all of which are larger than the self. Those strategic thoughts, however, don't magically turn men and women into saints. In the viper pit of politics, the bites have no less sting. In an era that has seen a melding of politics and celebrity—not to mention the phony familiarity cultivated on Facebook and Twitter—is there still a place for loyalty in politics?

It's worth looking at the overlap between America's two most visible cultures of ambition: DC and LA. For both popular stars and politicians, tending to an image is every bit important as—and perhaps more important than—a job itself. Without the image, there is no job. To be the female lead in a romantic comedy, it helps to be a charming, fit, girl-next-door. To be governor of Indiana, it helps to be a corn-fed, motorcycle-driving tough talker.

In both Hollywood and DC—worlds dominated by visual media—vibrant, youthful candidates have an undeniable edge. Qualities like competence and diligence? Those help, too. But all the brilliant policy making in the world couldn't do what one photo of a shirtless Barack Obama in the Hawaiian surf did for his presidential campaign in 2008.

For players in both cities, there are no "off" hours. To present themselves properly, they must eat at the right places, talk to the right media, and be photographed at the right events. Both cultures feed on the celebrity's or politician's need for acceptance, which is carefully masked by stratospheric levels of self-confidence.

Though principals in each town require a small army of assistants and helpers, Washington staffers are part of a discrete breed: highly visible public employees with cachet that exists only in context. They act as special advisors, policy directors, and legislative assistants for politicians who are the center of attention. Elected officials, to varying degrees, are cut off from the real world, often displaced from their homes and living near the Capitol. And so their staffers are sounding boards, go-betweens, and occasionally, at least in the case of this president, basketball opponents. Let's not forget that the term "body man," jargon for a politician's personal assistant who goes everywhere with and does nearly everything for him, is a Washington phenomenon.

Given the importance of staff, loyalty is crucial. But it is also challenged constantly by staff members' own desire for personal gain. From former White House Chief of Staff Rahm Emanuel, now running for mayor of Chicago, to the legions of press secretaries on the Hill, staff members have limitless opportunities to make good on their status. And while plenty of them are long-serving, hardworking, and tight-lipped, plenty of others—at every level of governance—leave their posts to share what they know in the form of books, articles, or tips to reporters.

What, then, is a politician to do? No one can run an office—and certainly not the next campaign—without a little help. One answer: bring in your friends. After all, why not rely on the people who care about you the most?

Trusted friends offer insulation from the extreme ups and downs of political life. Trouble is, politics can be a place where friendships go to die. With the demands of campaigning, the glare of media attention, and the responsibilities of office, there are countless ways a well-intentioned friend can unwittingly damage a political career.

Elected officials, unlike leaders of perhaps any other industry, need friends who possess above-average levels of integrity (which is not to say they always have them) for the simple reason that their friends can wind up on the public payroll. Hollywood might be able to tolerate bad behavior, but in Washington the taxpayers are footing the bill. Whatever flaws one has or mistakes one has made in the past will (or should) come under intense scrutiny sooner or later. Even if a friend is innocent of traits or behaviors with which he or she is associated, the story exists—and can be problematic. Ultimately, what a politician needs are not just good friends but good friends who are also unquestionably good people.

The White House is perhaps the most closely watched scene for the comings and goings of friends who become major characters in the narrative—for good or ill. Incoming administrations tend to rely heavily on an inner circle from home, at least at the beginning of a term. President Obama has his Chicago circle. President Bush was insulated by Texans. President Clinton had his Arkansas crowd.

The benefit of filling the White House with close friends is understandable and practical: they can give a president their valued opinions and help, as well as a connection to life before 1600 Pennsylvania Avenue.

But bringing in the home team doesn't always work out, as the case of Desirée Rogers, former White House social secretary to President Obama, demonstrated. Rogers, who was a longtime friend of the First Lady, brought a nontraditional approach to the job.

Not only did she engage less with the Washington insider circuit that previous social secretaries courted, she herself became a figure of media attention, if not fascination. She was profiled and featured in magazines. She made a splash at fashion shows in New York. At the White House state dinner for India, she wore a sheer, deconstructed dress by the label Comme Des Garcons—which would have been greeted with accolades in New York or Los Angeles. In DC, this bold fashion choice was considered something of a curiosity—and not entirely appropriate.

Rogers was in no way a behind-the-scenes player. The inside-the-Beltway narrative about Rogers soon focused on how she was upstaging her friend, the First Lady. And so, when it became known that a social-climbing couple, Tareq and Michaele Salahi, attended the state dinner without an invitation, Rogers came under heavy fire. The sensational story of the "crashers" dominated headlines for weeks and caused major embarrassment to the White House and the Secret Service. No matter who was to blame for the Salahis's entry into the executive mansion, the story took on a life of its own: it was the story of a spotlight-loving social secretary who had changed the procedures and was too busy attending the party to properly supervise it.

Rogers's stylishness and visible role stood in sharp contrast to that of White House senior advisor Valerie Jarrett, one of President Obama's oldest friends. With her executive background and demeanor, she fits—or accepts—the Washington mold. She's present at parties and social events, but not necessarily accessible. She engages with the media in a way that delivers the president's messages effectively. In her television interviews, she appears unflappable.

The difference between Rogers and Jarrett is not just a matter of personality. Washington doesn't bend. Rogers took risks and did it her way. Jarrett is a Washington type—or at least behaves like one. Both are dear friends of the Obamas and only one is still working for them.

For some politicians, the trouble with friends happens along the road to Washington. Vice-presidential candidate John Edwards had a trusted friend and longtime aide in Andrew Young. When Edwards engaged in an extramarital affair, it was natural for him to rely on Young, who dutifully covered Edwards's tracks. Until he didn't.

Young's tell-all book, *The Politician*, reveals all manner of ugly details about Edwards's romance with campaign videographer Rielle Hunter. When Hunter became pregnant, Edwards asked Young to prevent the truth from coming to light by claiming he was the father. In asking Young to engage in an epic endeavor of obfuscation, Edwards promised he would take care of Young—at least, that is what Young believed.

Young writes of the moment when Edwards laid out the idea: "He would make sure I had a job in the future, he said. 'You're family. A friend like no friend I've ever had,' he added before concluding that if I helped him, I would make Mrs. Edwards dying days a bit easier."

Help a friend—or escape with your reputation intact? Young's choice, a choice he viewed as driven by his personal loyalty to Edwards, made him virtually unemployable. And so when Young and his wife felt betrayed by the Edwardses, they had a trump card to play: write the book and set the record straight. Today neither Edwards nor Young is likely to be able to work in politics again.

What is surprising about their story isn't its portrait of friendship betrayed; it's the fact that their mutual duplicity stayed secret for as long as it did. Today it is all too common in American political life for once-devoted friends to become political liabilities—or even career-killers.

The Reverend Jeremiah Wright was a long-standing figure in the life of Barack Obama: the reverend officiated at the Obamas' wedding and baptized their two daughters. But Wright became a serious campaign problem in 2008 when his radical sermons circulated online via YouTube—followed by new controversial statements Wright made to defend himself. Obama was forced to publicly break from Wright and his church, saying, "He has done great damage, I do not see that relationship being the same."

It surely wasn't for Wright. His poignant comments to the *Washington Post* in March 2010 revealed clearly the unpleasant experience of being cast out of the charmed political circle: "I have not stopped loving him because of what the press did," Wright said. "And to see him beat up on because of things he is not responsible for is painful."

Another friendship that has most likely been severed for good is that between former New York City mayor Rudy Giuliani and the man he tapped to be New York City police commissioner, Bernard Kerik. In 2004 Giuliani put Kerik forward for the top post in the Bush administration's Department of Homeland Security. Just days later, Kerik withdrew as a nominee after an immigration problem with a former housekeeper and nanny arose. The issue would not have prevented him from making his way through the Senate confirmation process. But as it turned out, that was just the beginning.

In 2006 Kerik pled guilty in New York State court to two ethics violations and was ordered to pay a fine. Then in 2009 he pled guilty to tax fraud, lying on a loan application, and five counts of lying to the federal government. In February 2010 he was sentenced to four years in prison.

Every step of the way must have been especially embarrassing for Giuliani, who had been a champion and mentor to Kerik. At the time Kerik withdrew from White House consideration, the former mayor was building momentum for the Republican presidential primary. Giuliani's judgment and standards were called into question. But as the legal trouble mounted, it became clear that the ethics violations should have prevented him from rising to the post of police commissioner. Giuliani had promoted and recommended a man as public servant—several times over— either with or without full knowledge of Kerik's true character.

In any hiring situation, that knowledge is desirable. But in politics, especially when personal friends are involved, it is absolutely crucial. The politician's friend has a unique personal connection, but that connection is subject to public scrutiny.

It is this aspect of political friendship that makes Washington, DC's test for loyalty so much more stringent than LA's—and also why stories of disloyalty inside the Beltway are a bit less juicy than the latest catfight on *Real Housewives of New York*. If Kerik wasn't a public figure but merely a private businessman who enjoyed whisking his important friend around to power lunches and luxe vacation spots, he might still have landed himself in jail for fraud, but he wouldn't have violated the public's trust and torpedoed a political candidacy in the process. And he would have one more friend than he does now.

Part 2

Smells Like Teen Spirit

7: An Unnatural Habitat
The Separate Lives of Adolescence

Mark Bauerlein

FORTY YEARS AGO, if you were a fifteen-year-old caught up in customary concerns—friends, clothes, kissing, music—television didn't provide much germane material. If you lived in Atlanta and came home from school on May 18, 1970, here is what you would find at 3:00 p.m. Channel 2 presented *Another World*, channel 5 *The Secret Storm*, and channel 11 *General Hospital*, three soap operas a teen couldn't even consider. Channel 17 had *My Little Margie*, an *I Love Lucy*–type comedy from the 1950s with an eccentric twentysomething heroine who wore nice dresses and spoke proper English. Finally, Channel 36 broadcast *Rocket Robin Hood*, a cartoon for children.

That was it. Later hours offered game shows (*Truth or Consequences, To Tell the Truth*), a talk show (*Merv Griffin*), some silly comedies (*Gilligan's Island, The Munsters, My Favorite Martian*), and more kids' fare (*The Flintstones, Sesame Street, Clutch Cargo*). The only show focusing on teens was *Patty Duke* at 7 p.m. ("Patty promises that her father will address a creative writing class—without bothering to ask him first," *TV Guide* summarizes).

Compare that starvation diet of TV for teens with today's menu. A fifteen-year-old Atlantan hitting the "Power" button on a late April afternoon in 2010 could choose from:

> ► *My Super Sweet 16*—an MTV series profiling fabulously expensive birthday parties;

- *Malcolm in the Middle*;
- *Full House*—where the Olsen twins got their start, but with teenage girls in the cast as well;
- *Suite Life on Deck*—more twins, this time mid-teen boys;
- *Punk'd*—a *Candid Camera*–like show hosted by Ashton Kutcher, today's episode starring Jamie Lynn Di Scala, famous as the teenage daughter on *The Sopranos*;
- *Ferris Bueller's Day Off*—which seems to air once a month; and
- *My Boss's Daughter*—a 2003 film starring, once again, Ashton Kutcher.

Comcast Cable service also provides "On Demand" programming, on this day offering several more captivating shows and films for teens including:

- *After School*—a 2008 boarding school film;
- *Cutting Class*—another high school film (1989), murders included, with Brad Pitt; and
- *First Daughter*—from 2004, the president's daughter heads to college.

These productions don't just showcase adolescents working through teen angst or plotting hijinks while parents and teachers carry on with their duties. They impart a whole universe of experience, a complete habitat in which adolescent values and interests dominate. Grown-ups usually appear in two-dimensional versions, popping into the youth sphere as injunctions and irritants, coming from and returning to a grown-up realm that has all the appeal of a social studies textbook. No grandfather steps into a boy's bedroom to say, "Let me talk to you for a while about what Vietnam made us feel and think." A mother doesn't rebuke a wayward daughter who skips school and mocks learning with "Do you know that if *my* mother wanted to become a professional, she had two choices: nurse or teacher?" No allusions to taxes, corruption in government, venality in the marketplace, good and bad foreign leaders, twentieth-century ideologies, unemployment, Original Sin, or anything else dark and tragic in human history.

Instead, these programs raise ordinary fears and ambitions of the teen ego—Do I look okay? Do they like me? Am I invited? Can I get a car?—to dramatic, decisive standing. The very presence of youth on twelve different channels for hours every day and night grants a lasting validity and consequence to youth aims and anxieties even when the outcomes of the plots display their shortsightedness. If a teen movie such as *Bring It On* displays young girls behaving badly, teen viewers rank the moral lesson lower than the significance of full immersion precisely in the motives and desires of seventeen-year-old girls. They assume quite logically that they are supremely worthy of moral drama, and their dramatic status counts more than the moral judgment that follows.

In other words, the sheer volume of attention to adolescence, from the press of peers all day at school to the intake of peer images and sounds all evening at home, has its impact. It reinforces the adolescent outlook. It magnifies the happenings and anxieties that adolescents should transcend even as they experience and act upon them. Yes, it's great to be popular in eleventh grade, but it's also crucial to recognize that the things that make you popular in high school don't foster the virtues that make for adult success: discipline, studiousness, work ethic, knowledge. Of course, those things don't lend themselves to hour-long TV plotlines, and so they slide into tediousness in real life. Keep in mind that television viewing remains the lengthiest leisure activity for teens. The 2008 American Time Use Survey issued by the Bureau of Labor Statistics clocks fifteen- to nineteen-year-olds at 2.5 hours of TV on weekdays, 3.3 hours on weekend days, about half of their leisure time overall (reading tallies around 21 minutes a day). Kaiser Foundation's 2010 study of media use, *Generation M²: Media in the Lives of 8- to 18-Year-Olds*, gives "TV content" 4.5 hours a day, the next most popular media, "Music/audio," garnering 2.5 hours. How much does that total by age eighteen?

Add to teen TV time a host of digital practices oriented around peer-to-peer contact. Nielsen Company reported in January 2010 that teens with a mobile device send or receive 3,146 text messages per month, their intent nicely summarized in the subtitle of an April 2010 Pew Internet and American Life Project report: "Text messaging explodes as teens embrace it as the centerpiece of their communication strategies with friends." Regular voice calls remain central, too, Nielsen calculating two years ago that cell-wielding teens average 231 phone calls per month. Teens also like self- and friend photos, Pew finding that 64 percent of online teens share pictures back and forth through the cell phone alone. Meanwhile, social networking continues to increase; Pew reported in November 2006 that 55 percent of online teens use social media. In February 2008 Pew raised the tally to 65 percent, and then to 73 percent in February 2010.

Television, Facebook, iPhone, Photoshop, text messaging . . . they yield a whole new youth lifeworld. Or rather, they extend an old youth culture to every minute and every space of an adolescent's day and night. "Most youth use online networks to extend the friendships that they navigate in the familiar contexts of school, religious organizations, sports, and other local activities," say researchers in a MacArthur Foundation–supported study entitled *Living and Learning with New Media: Summary of Findings from the Digital Youth Project* (November 2008). "They can be 'always on,' in constant contact with their friends via texting, instant messaging, mobile phones, and Internet connections." They can plop into bed at midnight or lounge in the back of their parents' car while driving across New Mexico on Interstate 40 and conduct an up-to-the-minute social life. The bedroom used to be a secluded space, and parents could banish misbehaving kids to it as punishment. Today, "Go to your room—you're grounded!" is a laughable notion. Unless parents also confiscate the iPhone, TV set, and laptop, teens can still commiserate with pals blockaded in other bedrooms across town. Even when everything is turned off and unplugged, they feel the presence of peers, for they never know what text messages are waiting, photos have been posted, gossip is circulating through Facebook . . .

The problem extends beyond the overtly damaging practices such as cyber-bullying, sexting, adult predators, and gaming addictions. The fact that teenagers can tap representations of their age group at any time and in any place, that they can talk and write to and about one another voluminously by the hour, that they can broadcast so efficiently an LOL picture or juicy revelation from the previous night's party . . . such advents upset the delicate balance of peer influence and adult influence. The obvious and plain actuality of those new talents might obscure their impact, but they nonetheless expel voices and values that don't pertain to youth concerns.

Those concerns are mightily exclusionary. Fifty years ago James Coleman identified them as central to "the adolescent society," a high school zone of "separate subcultures . . . subcultures with languages all their own, with special symbols, and, most importantly, with value systems that may differ from adults" (*The Adolescent Society: The Social Life of the Teenager and Its Impact on Education*, 1961). Because high school creates such emphatic age-segregations to which contact with adults has no social import (what do teachers know?), teenagers develop their own rules and judgments, the respect of one another counting a lot more than the approval of parents. If you don't speak the language and share the values, the punishment is excruciating. You can't join the group, and so you have to mingle all day in class and hallways estranged and disesteemed, with nowhere else to go.

The values themselves, Coleman found in his studies of high school students, steer in predictable directions. When asked how they would like to be remembered in their schools, boys ranked "athletic star" and girls ranked "most popular" well above "brilliant student." When they listed the qualities that got people into the "leading crowd" in their schools, boys set personality, reputation (don't be a delinquent), athletics, and looks above academics, while girls placed personality, reputation (don't be a tramp), looks, clothes, and money above academics. Furthermore, when it came to charting what makes boys and girls attractive to the other sex, the trend shifted farther from academic and toward social virtues. Coleman's conclusion: "our society has within its midst a set of small teen-age societies, which focus teen-age interests and attitudes on things far removed from adult responsibilities."

Coleman's portrait explains why a limit to peer influence and youth culture is crucial to the growing-up process. The pull of adolescence, the blandishments of popularity, the trauma of isolation, teasing, shunning . . . few teenagers can withstand them on their own. They spend 190 days per year crowded into one building with one thousand others, shuffling from room to room, eating and jostling and jawing and exercising together. What counts more than the whispering glances of a group at the next table in the cafeteria? What hurts or enthralls more than a desired one agreeing or not to go to a movie? Certainly not a parent who chides, "Finish your homework!" Reputations rise and fall, fashions change quickly, tribes form and deform. The average teen can barely keep up. F. Scott Fitzgerald termed it "the drama of the shifting, semicruel world of adolescence" way back in 1920, applying it to a rarefied group of moneyed, prep-school kids. Today it touches almost every adolescent living above the poverty line.

As long as youth messages couldn't overwhelm the home, the car, the vacation spot, the classroom, and the library, parents and teachers exercised a critical mass of influence on the young. Kids had to heed talk about money, current events, home repairs, the past, and the future. They may have preferred *The Patty Duke Show*, but she usually lost out to her competitors in the time slot, news anchors Huntley/Brinkley and Walter Cronkite. They had

AM radio and what is now called the "land line," but the environment was balanced enough to impose upon them an adult society, a cognizance of grown-up matters however dull and inapt they seemed.

No longer. Nearly everyone has a mobile device, an e-mail account, a personal profile page. You can't have a social life without one, and to sustain you have to use it often and vigilantly. Mizuko Ito terms it a "hypersocial" lifestyle, and in such a habitat virtue falls far down the scale of preferred attributes. Adolescents set other criteria—looks, clothes, fame, athletics, technology—as they always have. Adolescents haven't changed, but the ingredients of their formation into adults have. The grown-up culture that more or less blunts and counters adolescent culture has slipped toward negligibility. Millennials don't reject their parents. They ignore them, passively so, usually without anger or disrespect, as they tune in their friends.

As a result, they take longer to mature, to outgrow the values of adolescence. They acquire adult attitudes in their twenties, not in their late teens. Whether they emerge at age thirty as responsible and virtuous as they would have if the maturing process had started earlier remains to be seen. But if young people do start to recognize adult matters and interests and virtues mostly *after* they leave the home, then parents play a diminished role in the passage from adolescence to adulthood. Each parent faces a new question: how much of a factor do you want to play in the kind of adult your child becomes?

8: The Achievement Trap
How Overparenting Undermines Character

Caitlin Flanagan

W HEN THEY COME for us, we'll be in good shape if the defining contest is anything that involves the trumpet. Or the SAT. Or even water polo. Children of the American achievement classes spend most of their adolescences preparing for one thing: getting into college. Their belief in the power of Duke and Cornell and Middlebury is akin to the Easter Islanders' belief in the power of the giant stone heads: no one knows where they came from, but everyone understands they must be revered. Nothing can persuade these kids otherwise, and they have become less like normal human teenagers—driven by impulse, attracted to risk, eager to prove themselves as deserving of adult status—and more like sideshow attractions, always trying to draw a crowd: here the bearded lady, there the seventeen-year-old with the four AP classes and the five-minute mile. Their harassing and exhausting extracurricular activities (perversely and invariably referred to as their "passions") may have been born of some half-forgotten bit of genuine pleasure but by the time they have been transubstantiated into the stuff of an Ivy admission they are just another part of the grind.

We know that these teenagers sacrifice a great deal to create these weird little résumés of achievement—losses of free time and of independence—but we are less willing to address the most significant of these losses: the knowledge that they are competent, useful, capable of taking care of themselves, and perhaps of others, if the chips ever come down. They are hobbled and child-like, deeply dependent on the parents who make their participation in the various belt-notching exercises possible. What they are really prepared to do, at the end of all this, is only one thing: to replicate the society that has created them. It's a closed system of test-takers and French horn players, capable only of creating more of themselves.

It wasn't always this way. In the weeks after the attack on Pearl Harbor, the young men of Harvard and Yale and Amherst and Duke enlisted in the armed services in droves; they did not know if they were the measure of what lay ahead, but they knew that to them (by virtue, in part, of the very privilege that had landed them in college) fell the responsibility of joining the cause. But September 11 saw the men and women of those elite institutions sitting put. Different times, different situations. Perhaps. But clearly there were two related ideas, neither of them having anything to do with America's foreign policy, keeping so many of those able-bodied, highly educated young people out of the recruiters' offices. The first was an arrogant assumption that they had more to offer their country in terms of their collective social capital than in terms of their physical service (what crazed nation would put in harm's way the young woman who had so recently starred in Oakwood High's production of *Ain't Misbehavin'*?); second that none of them was really . . . up for it. What does a child whose greatest act of bravery thus far had been the decision to go Early Action know of courage under fire?

That these deep questions about their worth, and about the point of their entire enterprise, deeply rankle millions of middle- and upper middle-class American adolescents is proven by the emergence of a wildly popular new niche in the young adult fiction market, which might be called survival lit. A typical novel of this genre concerns a teenager or a small group of teenagers who, because of force majeur, have been thrust into an uncaring world, one in which the adults are either absent or feckless and in which the struggle for food, shelter, and safety is a constant. This, essentially, is the story of Terry Pritchard's best-selling *Nation*, a book about a teenage boy and girl who for reasons too baroque to explain—tidal wave, influenza, wrinkle in time—find themselves the last two people on Earth, left alone to bury the dead, forage for food, and restart the world.

Obviously, this is not the first literary moment in which stories of this kind have been attractive to young readers uncertain about their fitness for a world not controlled and regulated by parents. The granddaddy of the genre, *The Lord of the Flies*, was published more than fifty years ago, and from its earliest pages the uselessness of an effete education in matters of life and death emerges as a major concern.

Before we meet our hero, Ralph—fair-haired, fit, stunned to have crash-landed onto this unnamed tropical island—he has already taken off his school sweater; he is trailing it behind him in the novel's beautiful opening scene. What use the colors and insignia of the public school in no-man's-land? When we meet his nemesis, Jack, the boy is pompously and ridiculously wearing the black cloak and golden badge of the school's choir, one of several honors that he believes renders him the obvious leader of the group of lost boys: "I ought to be chief," said Jack with simple arrogance, 'because I'm chapter chorister and head boy. I can sing C sharp." But it's Ralph who is elected by acclaim, Ralph who sees the boys' ability to survive their situation devolving from something larger and less childish than the rituals and honors of their school—decency, honor, the ability to behave in a nonsavage way—"We're English, and the English are best at everything. So we've got to do the right things."

Today's novels of adolescent survival are the grandchildren of *The Lord of the Flies*, and none of them is as popular as *The Hunger Games*, the first of a trilogy by Suzanne Collins, that at present writing has spent a consecutive eighty-one weeks on the *New York Times'* best seller list.

The Hunger Games became known to me during the summer

of 2009, when I was compelled by my then eleven-year-old son Conor—who had just closed the book in a shudder of horrified excitement and literary satisfaction—to take the next exit off the freeway (we were en route from Los Angeles to San Francisco) so that we could immediately locate a bookstore and acquire volume two. I'm no pushover, but this was apparently some kind of emergency, and within half an hour we were standing in the Carmel Valley Borders receiving the devastating news: it would not be published for another twelve weeks. It was of some relief to me to discover that Conor's reaction was hardly unique: all across America children were in fits of agony and suspense awaiting the next installment of this blockbuster series.

Here is what they knew so far: in a postapocalyptic, deeply corrupt America—divided, by the tyrants at its helm, into twelve districts—the people are kept in check and in fear by an annual, televised contest called *The Hunger Games.* These exercises consist of the selection of two adolescents from each district, who are trained and fattened in the sinister capital, and then abandoned in an unforgiving wilderness to kill or be killed. The sole survivor is declared the winner, made a celebrity, and his or her family is relieved of the hard labor and chronic hunger that are the lot of the citizenry.

Our heroine is a sixteen-year-old girl named Katniss Evergreen, who has lived with her mother and younger sister in the most desolate and hardscrabble of the nation's twelve provinces, where the only industry is coal mining and where it is not uncommon for people to starve to death. Her father has been killed in a mine explosion, one that has rendered her mother all but mute: to Katniss has fallen the job of providing for the little family, which she does by sneaking outside the perimeter of her district and hunting wild game. That she has been transformed into a much harder creature than the typical reader is established early on: she reveals, brazenly, that she once considered drowning her sister's pet cat.

The novel opens on the morning of the Reaping, which is the day when the participants in that year's games are to be chosen, more or less at random, but with a twist—during the long, hungry year that leads up to the Reaping, adolescents can earn extra food for their families by increasing their own risk: if they enter their name in the lottery multiple times they are paid a small sum, and Katniss, it turns out has done just that, but still she escapes selection; it is her beloved little sister, Primrose, whose name gets called, and so Katniss makes a second sacrifice, offering herself in Prim's place and heading off to the games. Suffice it to say, she goes, she wins, and she really does kill several other teenagers along the way.

It's easy to see why adolescents are so attracted to this story. In the first place, it's macabre and gory, and it describes a world of extreme physical privation, which is always of deep interest to children. But it also suggests that a teenager is capable of making a real contribution to others using only her wits, and sometimes nothing more than the simple, physical fact of her existence: by accepting the extra tesserae, literally bargaining with her life, she has served her mother and sister.

Like *The Lord of the Flies*, *The Hunger Games* gives us a world of teenagers, left to their own devices and required to prove their mettle not in the cosseted world of school, but in the brutal world of the wilderness. But there are several important differences between the two novels. In *The Lord of the Flies*, the adults are well and truly absent. The children constantly wonder what "grown-ups" would do if they were in their situation, and both Ralph's and Jack's actions are constantly grounded in either an emulation or a rejection of the grown-up codes they have learned back home, which by turn seem essential and utterly trivial to successful life on the island. But in *The Hunger Games* the adults are always watching—secret cameras record every moment, every freezing night, desperate day, or squalid killing. In fact, the point of the games, largely, is to entertain the adults, and much of what Katniss does (because of a complex system of sponsorship and voting, one that can skew the results in her favor) is to curry the favor of the audience at home. Just as important, the nature of the games is to pit each and every child against one another; all but one must be killed so that one can win. Although society continually breaks down— ultimately disastrously so—in *The Lord of the Flies* there is always hope that Ralph, with his notions of democracy and decency, can prevail among the boys, and a community can by created.

These two precepts constitute the unlovely and inescapable essentials of the elite college-bound teenager's life. The first is the suspicion that one of the principal reasons for their relentless competition is the entertainment and betterment of adults. The college admissions industrial complex is big business; the College Board alone, which is charged with making some of the first, crudest discernments among the throng, employs thousands of people. More important, the parents of all of these overweening kids are emotionally involved with their pursuit to an unseemly and probably unhealthy degree. Most of these teenagers are terrified of disappointing their parents, and for that they have misspent a huge part of their unrecoverable youth. Pitted against one another, playing in the zero-sum game of gaining admission to colleges that can't take as many kids as want to attend, the dream time of youth forfeited for the Ritalin-charged hypertime of SAT cram sessions, the one thing they can never escape are the hopes and expectations of Mom and Dad, who are always tuned into the games.

In the last chapter of *The Lord of the Flies*, the boys are rescued by an officer of the Royal Navy. He is disgusted to see how they have behaved, and what they have become, and he tells them as much, in a haunting echo of Ralph's earlier assertion—"I should have thought that pack of British boys—you're all British, aren't you?—would have been able to put up a better show than that."

But then the boys break down and begin crying, and in the final, memorable image of the novel the officer, "moved and a little embarrassed," turns his back on them. It's the one thing that the adults of *The Hunger Games* and of our current crop of adolescents will never do: look away from their children, give them the requisite privacy to pull themselves together, to summon something deep within themselves, to become grown-ups themselves.

Part 3

At Your Leisure

9: Games People Play—Together

Jonathan V. Last

ONCE UPON A TIME, Robert Putnam was worried about bowling. The Harvard sociologist noticed that between 1960 and 2000, the number of Americans who bowl increased, while the number of people who bowl in leagues decreased. The result, Putnam believed, that people were, as he titled his influential book, *Bowling Alone*. His worry was that the tendency to bowl alone was a symptom of declining sociability, which led to declining civic participation, which would lead, eventually, to a general decline in the quality and vigor of American society.

Putnam might be buoyed by the rise of video-game bowling. In 2006 Nintendo launched a home video-game console called the Wii, unlike any video-game system ever made. Where all previous video games were controlled by tiny joysticks and buttons, the Wii uses a mimetic (motion-sensing) controller. The slim, white device looks like a small TV remote. You hold it in your hand and then simply *do* whatever you want to do onscreen. For instance, if you are playing a tennis game, whenever you want to hit the ball, you swing your arm as you would in real tennis.

The Wii's unique controller begs for a certain type of game: simple, tactile, and—surprisingly—social. Not long ago I had a house full of family for the weekend. It was a large group, ranging from my twenty-eight-year-old, hipster brother to my eighty-three-year-old Uncle Walter. After dinner one night we brought out the

Wii. Uncle Walter had never touched a video game, but he figured out the controls in about ninety seconds. A minute later the eight of us were bowling. Four hours (and a couple bottles of wine) later, we were all still talking, laughing, and playing. It was one of the most pleasantly sociable nights my family has ever had.

The Wii has been a revolutionary success, changing the shape of the video-game industry and turning video games into a high-order social diversion. But it was not always thus. In fact, it was once quite the opposite. In 1982 Surgeon General C. Everett Koop claimed that video games were responsible for many obvious "aberrations in childhood behavior." In 1997 the game *Grand Theft Auto* became a controversy because it put players in control of a criminal whose goal was to cause as much murder and mayhem as possible. Extra points were awarded, for instance, if your player killed innocent bystanders. Double points were awarded if you did so by running them over with a stolen police car. After Eric Harris and Dylan Klebold's 1999 shooting rampage at Columbine High School, their behavior was partly explained by their obsession with video games, including the hyperviolent game *Doom*.

The Wii signals a rejection of all of that. Games for the Wii tend to be activity based: tennis, bowling, golf. They are also designed to be played in large groups. (Many Wii games actually feature a dedicated "party mode.") All of which made the Wii a sensation: in just three years it sold nearly 68 million consoles, outselling its two rivals, the Microsoft Xbox 360 and Sony Playstation 3, combined. The story of video games is interesting because it shows how malleable technology is. We never know how a society will develop its technological geegaws. The Aztecs, for instance, invented the wheel but never used it as anything but a children's toy. In America video games actually began as harmless diversions, but they developed into a very real social ill. It is only by a stroke of very good fortune that they are actually returning to their roots and becoming once more a source of low-level social virtue.

In a single generation the video game permeated American life. In 1970 just a handful of people knew what a video game was. Today 68 percent of Americans play video games, an astonishing rise. Video games began in the defense industry in the late 1960s when early computer geeks used military-grade supercomputers to run simple games, such as Computer Space. The first publicly available game appeared in a California bar, Andy Capp's Tavern, in September of 1972. It was called *Pong.*

A simple game mimicking table tennis, *Pong* allowed two players to twist knobs, which controlled "paddles" on a television screen, enabling them to "bounce" a ball back and forth. The game was created by Al Alcorn and Nolan Bushnell, who had just founded a tiny start-up company called Atari. Alcorn and Bushnell put the jerry-rigged device on top of an old wine barrel. It worked like a pinball machine: the players put a quarter in the slot and then played until someone won the match. The instructions for the game read, in toto, "Avoid missing ball for high score."

Two weeks after they installed the game, Alcorn received a call from a bartender at Andy Capp's. "This is the weirdest thing," he said. "When I opened the bar this morning, there were two or three people at the door waiting to get in. They walked in and played the machine. They didn't buy anything. I've never seen anything like this before." By 1973 Atari had orders for 2,500 Pong machines; by the end of 1974, they had sold 8,000. (According to Scott Cohen's corporate biography of Atari, the machines were earning $200 per week, real money in the early 1970s.)

At the same time, Magnavox introduced a crude home video-game console, the Odyssey. As Steven Kent reports in his *Ultimate History of Video Games*, the runaway success of Pong whetted people's appetites for the video game, helping the Odyssey sell 85,000 units in its first year of release.

It's fitting that the first video games were both simple and social. Even more than the pinball machine, they commanded interaction between both players and the audience they attracted.

They were rudimentary enough that anyone could figure them out. Most important, they were designed to be multiplayer. You played with a friend, never against "the computer." In a philosophical sense, early video games were indistinguishable from billiards, darts, or bowling. They were simply another means of fomenting sociability. As the *Los Angeles Times* wrote in a 1974 article about the video-game craze sweeping the nation, "never before has an amusement game been so widely accepted by all ages. Everyone from teenagers to senior citizens enjoy the challenge that the Video Games offer."

Atari led the industry with games such as *Gotcha* (one of the first racing games) and *Steeple Chase* (where players jumped horses over gates). Rival game-maker Midway released the first violent game, *Gunfight,* in which two players controlled cowboys who shot at each other. What all of these early games shared was their universal appeal and interactivity—you played a game everyone understood and you played it *with* someone else.

By 1976 the industry was beginning to change. Exidy Games released a game called *Death Race.* It was still multiplayer—you and a friend each controlled a race car driving around a track—only now the object was to run over tiny stick figures. The game-maker called these figures "gremlins," but it was generally understood that they were people. *Death Race* was controversial enough to be mentioned on *60 Minutes.*

In 1978 *Space Invaders* became the first widely successful game to be imported from Japan, and it changed forever the way video games were understood. Unlike nearly all of the American games, *Space Invaders* was based on a story—that aliens were invading and that the player was defending against them. The player played alone, shooting at this alien horde. There was no way to "win" the game since the aliens kept coming, wave after wave, until the player's three lives were exhausted. *Space Invaders* demanded that a player ignore his surroundings and focus on the game itself. Instead of facilitating social interaction, as other games had done, *Space Invaders* became a black hole for sociability. And with lemminglike aliens as the opponent, the machine became both adversary and playmate, dismissing the need for any sort of human interaction at all. Suddenly, video games were less like bowling and more like onanism. If the first days of video games were the Garden of Eden, *Space Invaders* was the apple from the tree of knowledge.

Space Invaders was staggeringly successful. In just one year 60,000 machines were sold in the United States—in bars, pizza parlors, restaurants, and even drugstores. After being purchased for an initial price of $1,700, the game could earn its owner up to $400 a week. With returns like that, suddenly an entire establishment catering solely to video games became a viable proposition. The arcade was born.

The arrival of *Space Invaders* began what is known—mistakenly, I would argue—as the Golden Age of video games. *Space Invaders* was followed by other extraordinarily popular, influential games, such as *Asteroids, Centipede, Pac-Man*, and *Donkey Kong*. Video games appeared everywhere, from movie theaters to convenience stores, even from funeral parlors to doctors' offices. And the arcade proliferated throughout the malls of suburban America.

Arcades had existed for decades. Typically set in dense, urban locales they originally featured nickelodeons and mechanical games. But in the late 1970s and early 1980s, video arcades mushroomed across the country. These new establishments were typically dark, crowded, and packed with video-game cabinets. If the first video games had been indistinguishable from any other number of pub-style entertainments, the arcade helped transform, and ghettoize, the video game into an activity with a much narrower appeal.

In the arcade the video game wasn't something one could do *while* socializing. It was the entire reason for being there in the first place. Where the early video games had required two or more people to play together, almost all of the video games from the Golden Age pitted single players against the computer, eliminating the need for companionship. And while the pub had assured that people of many ages would be around the video games, the arcade brought the video game to teens and adolescents, whose presence drove away adults. The arcade narrowed the core audience of video games to a younger, mostly male, demographic. (Video games's Golden Age is said to have ended in 1982 with the release of *Ms. Pac-Man*, the most successful game in the history of the industry, which sold 115,000 units in the United States alone.)

As arcades flourished, a raft of gaming consoles appeared, from Magnavox's second effort (the Odyssey2) to systems from Atari, Coleco, and Mattel, which brought video games into the home. These machines were most often sold in toy stores and played not even by teens, but by younger children, which moved video games farther away from the social mainstream. Even more unfortunately, the home consoles created a generation of children who grew up thinking it was normal to spend hours alone in front of a television, gripping a joystick. These devices were, in the most literal sense, antisocial.

But at least in the 1980s, it was the practice of gaming that was worrisome, not the games themselves. That would change.

In May 1992 programmers John Carmack and John Romero released a game called *Wolfenstein 3D*. It was revolutionary in a number of ways. First, Carmack and Romero had figured out a new way to render polygons with the computer, meaning that they were able to create three-dimensional spaces within a video-game world. Second, *Wolfenstein 3D* placed players in the body of the game's protagonist as he ran around a castle shooting enemies, so that only the protagonist's gun, bobbing at the bottom of the screen, was visible. This convention established an entirely new genre, which came to be known as the "first-person shooter."

But perhaps most important, *Wolfenstein 3D* introduced extreme violence and gore to the video game. Players shot Nazi soldiers (and their guard dogs) with a variety of guns. The soldiers' bodies flew apart as they were riddled with bullets. Blood sprayed against the walls and pooled on the floor. Entrails were sometimes visible spilling from the bodies. When players succeeded in killing one of the level-ending "boss" characters, the game rewarded them with a "Death Cam," which replayed the victorious confrontation like a sports-highlight reel. In his book about Carmack and Romero, *Masters of Doom*, David Kushner explains that the Death Cam was the programmers' "version of a snuff film."

Wolfenstein was a cult hit and it inspired Carmack and Romero to create *Doom*, a follow-up that was substantially similar to *Wolfenstein 3D*, only bloodier. Released in 1993, *Doom* was, like *Wolfenstein 3D*, made to be played on personal computers. By 1995 it had been installed on more than 10 million PCs.

During the 1990s arcades dwindled as home computers and video-game consoles became more powerful. They became capable of as much—and eventually even more—graphical sophistication as the stand-alone cabinet machines in arcades. By 1985 a new generation of consoles was being released every five years or so, with various corporations competing for dominance within each new wave. As home video-game consoles became cheaper and more powerful, they became more popular, drawing Nintendo, Sega, NEC, Sony, and eventually Microsoft into the market. It wasn't hard to see why: by 2004 video-game consoles had become a $10 billion-a-year business. In terms of raw dollar grosses, they now rival the film industry.

In a sense, this represented a re-expansion of the video game's audience: now, not only were children and adolescents playing games, but twenty- and thirtysomethings who had grown up during the Golden Age of video games were playing, too. Influenced by *Wolfenstein 3D* and *Doom*, the games they were playing became more complex and immersive. Instead of batting a ball back and forth between two paddles, or eating dots while traversing a maze, video games created entire worlds for players to explore.

Some of these worlds were as mindlessly violent as *Doom*. In the 1998 hit *Resident Evil 2*, for instance, players run around shooting zombies in the head, with little rhyme or reason. (Except that all zombies need shooting, QED.) Others, such as the aforementioned *Grand Theft Auto* series, mixed violence with prurience. In each iteration of *Grand Theft Auto*, players are placed in the shoes of a new villain in a new city and encouraged to work their way up the criminal hierarchy by killing, stealing, selling drugs, and so on and so forth.

Some games strived to be more middle-brow. The 2007 game *Bioshock*, for example, was a first-person shooter that attempted to explore the tensions between freedom and choice in Ayn Rand's objectivist philosophy. The catch is that *Bioshock* pursued this conversation with a game in which players run around an underwater city killing genetically engineered monsters and little girls.

What all of these games had in common, however, was their impetus toward isolation. The games were vast—many of them taking forty or more hours to complete—and they were designed to be played by one person at a time. A stereotype emerged of the video-game player as a grungy post-adolescent, alone in front of the TV in his apartment or, worse, his parents' basement. This stereotype was often close to the mark. As Tom Bissell notes in his video-game memoir *Extra Lives*, "Rarely has wide-ranging familiarity with a medium so transparently privileged the un- and under employed."

Bissell's musings about sitting for hours (and sometimes days) at a time with video games paint a particularly disturbing picture. An accomplished writer—he is a contributor to *Harper's* and the *New Yorker* with five books and several prestigious literary fellowships to his name—Bissell wrote in *Extra Lives*, "These days, I play video games in the morning, play video games in the afternoon, and spend my evenings playing video games. . . . Today, the most consistently pleasurable pursuit in my life is playing video games." Not implausibly, Bissell likens video games—the deep-world, first-person shooters such as *Grand Theft Auto* and *Bioshock* and *Resident Evil*—to cocaine. Both are isolating, insubstantial, and ultimately addictive.

All of which makes the sudden reemergence of the video game as a *social* pastime even more remarkable.

Nintendo had been a leader in the video-game world for nearly twenty years before falling on hard times in the late 1990s. Their video-game consoles were surpassed in popularity by Sony and Microsoft, who built machines that were increasingly powerful, making them capable of rendering ever larger, more complicated virtual worlds. Having been beaten in this technological arms race, Nintendo opted out and decided to make an entirely different kind of video game. Their model was *Pong*.

In 2004 Nintendo announced that they were working on a system code-named "Revolution." By the time it was released in late 2006, the system had been renamed the "Wii." Even the name was meant to signify its social aspect. Here was one press release: "Wii will break down that wall that separates game players from everybody else. Wii will put people more in touch with their games . . . and each other." Its success took the industry by surprise.

The Wii's competition was a pair of high-powered systems, the Microsoft Xbox 360 and Sony Playstation 3, which were designed to power sprawling, immersive, single-player games, like *Bioshock* and *Grand Theft Auto*. The Wii went in an entirely different direction. It had a low-power, previous-generation processor. All of Nintendo's research and development efforts went into creating a new kind of controller—a motion-sensing device that gave players physical command over games. The idea was to lower the barrier to entry for game-play, making the Wii so easy and intuitive that a sixty-eight-year-old grandmother would feel just as home with it as a fifteen-year-old boy.

Nintendo also simplified the type of game it made for the Wii, deciding to put forward short, social games meant to be played in groups. Instead of shooting zombies by yourself, the Wii was designed to get you playing doubles tennis with a crew of friends. Suddenly the video game was being used as it had been in the beginning—as another social facilitator, an intergenerational amusement indistinguishable in function from hearts or croquet or Robert Putnam's beloved bowling.

People have gone mad for the Wii. So far it has sold more than 26 million units in the United States, more than 68 million world-wide. It has sold more than the Xbox 360 and Playstation 3 put together. It is on pace to sell more consoles than any video-game system in history. The Wii effect has widened the demographic contours of gaming. Twenty-five percent of Americans over fifty now occasionally play video games and 44 percent of gamers are now women.

It is important to note that the Wii did not create this market. It tapped an appetite for social entertainment that has existed since the early days of video games, but which the industry slowly turned its back on over the years.

Our amusements are important. They provide vehicles for sociability, which is a small, but dear, good. Sociability provides the fuel for community and, ultimately, civil society. This is not to argue that video games will save the Republic. It is, however, encouraging that after years of tearing at the social fabric, the video game has once again become part of the tapestry of Ameri-can sociability, another thread that helps bind us together.

But perhaps the most encouraging aspect of today's video games is that they present an example of a technology that worked its way down a blind alley—and then, all on its own, found its way back out, into the light.

10: Unsportsmanlike Conduct

Why Pro Athletes Aren't Heroes

Joe Queenan

PROFESSIONAL SPORTS ARE wonderful diversions, but they teach us almost nothing about sportsmanship, morality, or character. Soccer is the most popular sport in the world, yet the 2010 World Cup was an epidemic of cheating. The Germans cheated, the Italians cheated, the Uruguayans cheated, and the Argentines really cheated. This was hardly a surprise; the coach of the Argentine team is the most famous cheater in the history of the sport, having scored the winning goal in the 1986 final against England by punching the ball into the net with his hand. The score is famously referred to as "The Hand of God" goal, an insult to both God and the English.

Soccer is only the most obvious example of a sport that teaches us very little that is useful in shaping character, other than to play hard and never give up. Playing hard and never giving up are generic lessons that can be learned elsewhere, most obviously from any working mother. Working mothers do not cheat. Football teams do. The New England Patriots stopped winning Super Bowls after they got caught secretly videotaping their opponents' practices. Three-point victors over the St. Louis Rams, the Carolina Panthers, and the Philadelphia Eagles, the heavily favored Patriots were emasculated by the New York Giants in the 2007 Super Bowl, the biggest upset in the history of the sport. Without knowing what their opponents were likely to do on defense, the

Patriots simply fell apart. The most prolific offense in the history of the sport, they now found themselves in a situation where they simply could not score. No video camera, no glory.

Cheating is a cornerstone of most professional sports, none more so than baseball. Steroid use is all about cheating: building up body mass artificially so that you can hit the ball harder, faster, longer, while recovering from injuries more quickly. But cheating has been a part of the game since the early part of the twentieth century, when legendary managers would bet against their own teams, and then rig the games in such a way that their teams lost. (The generally accepted practice of betting against your own team stopped after the Chicago White Sox en masse threw the 1919 World Series. That was just too outrageous.) We now know that when New York Giant Bobby Thomson belted his famous pennant-winning home run in a 1951 playoff game against the Brooklyn Dodgers—"the shot heard round the world"—he knew in advance what pitch Dodger hurler Ralph Branca was going to throw because the Giants were using a clubhouse telescope and a buzzer system to steal the catcher's signs and relay them to the batter. More recently, the league-leading Philadelphia Phillies got caught stealing signs from the catcher in a game against the Colorado Rockies, this time thanks to a coach armed with binoculars way out in the bullpen. The Phillies subsequently lost seventeen of their next twenty-five games. The implication was clear: when you cheat, you win; when you get caught cheating, you lose. Until proven otherwise.

Americans profess to love the underdog, but they usually don't start loving him until the underdog is already up by three touchdowns with less than two minutes left to play. The truth is, most fans support the teams that are most likely to win—the Los Angeles Lakers, Manchester United, Duke University, the Roman Empire—because it is human nature to shun the hapless and align oneself with the powerful. This is why one so rarely sees teenagers bedecked in Houston Astros regalia or sporting Los Angeles Clippers jerseys. It is also the reason voters who describe themselves as "independent" are most likely to vote for the party that seems destined to win anyway.

The most popular team in the history of professional sports is the New York Yankees. The Yankees vastly outspend their rivals and pile up championship after championship primarily because other teams cannot field squads of equal or even comparable talent. The Yankees routinely field magnificent teams, because magnificent teams are what $200 million will buy you. By contrast, $55 million will buy you the Kansas City Royals. Except in the minds of addled sportswriters, who indefatigably equate success with heroism, character never enters into this conversation. The Yankees, both individually and collectively, may possess superior moral character, but they do not win because of it. If superior character was what decided baseball games, gifted players like Alex Rodriguez and Mark Teixeira would have won championships before they started spending their summers in the Bronx. But these players did not win in Atlanta, Seattle, Fort Worth, and Anaheim, not because they lacked moral fiber but because they lacked teammates who could throw, catch, or hit the ball with any degree of power, precision, or regularity.

For reasons that are not clear, but which probably involve social class, there are sports where cheating is not tolerated. This is primarily in single-combat events where cheating is more obvious than in team sports, sports where you can trip people without anybody noticing. Golfers rarely cheat, or do tennis players. On the occasions when they do cheat—as Justine Henin did in a 2003 French Open semifinal match against Serena Williams, when she lied about having held up her hand to stop play during her opponent's first serve—a stigma remains that never really goes away. It would be nice if all professional sports had a code of honor like this, but they do not. There is too much money at stake and too much glory, and the truth is that many professional athletes have been cheating at sports since they were children. Hockey players kick in goals with their feet and try to give the opposing team's best player a concussion. Football players gouge, kick, trip, spit, garrote, and aim their helmets at their adversaries' knees. Tour de France bicyclists use drugs. Lots and lots of drugs. None of this is in any way character building.

This is not to say that all great sportsmen are cheaters. Nor is it to deny that there are events in sports history that are imbued with a powerful inspirational component, regardless of the outcome of the contest. Lou Gehrig's 1939 farewell speech at Yankee Stadium, where he refused to bellyache about the illness that would kill him two years later, is a perfect example. Speed skater Dan Jansen taught the world a thing or two about overcoming adversity when he won an Olympic gold medal in 1994 in the very last Olympic event he would ever skate in. This came after two disastrous performances in previous Winter Olympics contests, most memorably 1988 when he fell apart after learning by phone that his sister Jane was dying of leukemia. Ben Hogan, after a head-on collision with a Greyhound bus in 1949, came back to win the 1950 U.S. Open golf tournament. His legs were wrapped in bandages, and he had to win the tournament in a grueling eighteen-hole, three-way playoff. He did not knock in the winning putt with his hand.

Classiness is a separate issue, especially when it is so subtle as to be almost imperceptible. A couple of years after Muhammad Ali defeated Sonny Liston for the heavyweight championship of the world, Ali gave a nice payday to Zora Foley, a thirty-four-year-old, washed-up heavyweight who had never gotten a chance to fight for the title in his prime because the reigning champion Floyd Patterson deliberately ducked him. Foley entered the ring with no chance of defeating Ali, but at least he would be able to tell his grandchildren that he had once duked it out with the greatest boxer of them all and taken home the biggest paycheck of his career. By scheduling this otherwise extraneous bout, Ali was in effect paying tribute to all the gallant warriors that inspired him.

Ali's detractors often dismiss him as arrogant and cruel (which he most certainly was in the case of Sonny Liston, Joe Frazier, and George Foreman). But in honoring a superb heavyweight who had been cheated out of his day in the sun, Ali showed himself to be as generous a sportsman as anyone who ever entered the ring.

Incidents like this are rare. By and large you should not teach your children to imitate professional athletes when they are growing up unless you are absolutely determined to have professional athletes in the family. The workplace, for most people, is an environment that thrives on compromise and learning to get along with other people and not going out of your way to humiliate adversaries. It is the exact opposite of the world of professional sports. Athletes who have played at a high level hate to lose to anyone, anywhere, and will use every tactic available to make sure they win. They will do this regardless of the sport or the level of competition, because they hate to finish second in anything: football, billiards, Old Maids. If you happen to be at a company picnic softball game or a pickup basketball game and a retired professional athlete somehow gets involved, you will quickly discover that an athlete will not take it easy on you just because you are outclassed or because this is supposed to be a friendly match. Instead, he will pummel you. Ordinary people don't do this. There is an unwritten law in pickup basketball, as played by scrubs and weekend warriors, that you do not keep posting up the little guy and scoring easy baskets in the paint just because you happen to have a ridiculous height advantage. It's not sportsmanlike and it wrecks the game for everyone else. But real athletes will do this sort of thing all night long. Real athletes will size you up as a runt and spend the entire night verbally reminding you that you are a runt. Athletes have no concept of shame and even less of a sense of occasion. Athletes will block shots by scrawny teenagers. Athletes will dunk over midgets. Athletes will prey on the young and humiliate the old. Athletes only care about winning. They're not particular about who they're winning against.

This is where the role of the ringer comes in. A couple of years ago, PBS's designated mystic Deepak Chopra held an invitational golf tournament in Ojai, California. Chopra himself is a passionate, though incompetent, golfer. On the final day of the tournament, Chopra participated in a foursome that included Tina Mickelson, a professional golfer whose brother Phil is the second-best player on the pro tour today. The group was playing "best ball," in which each player keeps his—or her—own score and the best score for the hole goes onto the scorecard. That night, when the winning team was announced at an informal banquet, Chopra—not Mickelson—shamelessly strode forward to accept the trophy. Everything we do not want our children to learn about sportsmanship and class is contained in this anecdote. We do not want our children to win because the fix was in. We do not want our children to pass off somebody else's achievements as their own. And if they do insist on giving themselves a huge tactical advantage over the competition, we at least expect them to avoid acting surprised when the final score is announced, as if the outcome was ever in doubt. This is yet another reason why we should not encourage our children to emulate Deepak Chopra.

College basketball is stupefyingly popular in the United States, but not because of the quality of play. The crummiest bench-warmer on the worst team in the National Basketball Association is more talented than most college basketball players; scrubs who never get into the game in the pros were once vaunted collegiate All-Americans. But college basketball, as opposed to the professional version, appeals to Americans for reasons that have little to do with the ability of the performers. One, the games tend to be fairly competitive because all of the dominant players are already in the pros and the remaining talent is distributed relatively equally among fifty-some schools. Two, college basketball teams are loaded with hardworking strivers, ordinary kids who do not have the gifts or instincts to play in the pros. (There may also be a racial component at work here, as the NCAA "March

Madness" finals are the last time a Caucasian fan is going to get to see a bunch of skinny white kids competing for a championship.) Three, and perhaps most important, basketball fans feel a certain emotional kinship with college hoopsters, because the players dive for loose balls, and lay it all on the line, and never seem to be coasting the way the pros do. In the college basketball game of the mind, this is where ordinary fans see themselves. A nation of hardworking guys diving for loose balls. A nation of lunch-pail heroes.

Never mind that many of the top college players take bogus classes and accept no-show jobs and get money under the table from alumni. What is important here is a reassuring sense of realism among the fans themselves. At a certain level, unless they are completely delusional, fans understand that they could never return Roger Federer's return, could never get solid wood on a ball thrown by Mariano Rivera, would perish on the spot if Mike Tyson landed a right hook to their jaw. College basketball, by contrast, nourishes plausible daydreams. College basketball players seem like mortals. Most people who have been to a college of any consequence have crossed paths with college basketball players. They know that they could never beat these players in a game. But they might at least be able to score. By contrast, in a game against LeBron James, the average person would never get to take a shot. LeBron would take all of them. Thus, fans who despise professional basketball despise it precisely because the players in the National Basketball Association are too talented. Professional basketball is the only sport I can think that a good number of people avoid or at least deride because they view talent itself as a detriment. A case can further be made that college basketball purists are not especially sophisticated. This is the case that is being made here. I find college basketball positively lethal. I don't eat second-class food or look at second-rate paintings or read second-rate books. So why should I watch a dull, predictable, second-rate sport? Duke always ends up winning, anyway.

Anyone in his right mind knows that professional athletes possess skills that are not comparable to the skills ordinary people possess. Professional athletes are phenomenally good at what they do; the ordinary person, through no fault of his own, does nothing phenomenally well. That's why he is ordinary. The same is true of professional musicians or dancers or actors or politicians: a normal person cannot understand how a professional responds to certain situations because a normal person has never been put into a situation where a preposterous level of skill is required. Not at work. Not at play. Not even in the home. This, in the end, is why it is so hard to learn anything from professional sportsmen, because nothing in everyday life is analogous to the life of a professional athlete.

At least not on the playing surface. But occasionally, far away from the playing surface, you can learn something. Consider this: hockey players routinely smash each other into the boards, jam their sticks into opponents' faces, punch out the opponents' lights, knock out their teeth. But then in the TV interviews between periods, you will never hear a hockey player say anything bad about an opponent.

"It got a little chippy out there," a hockey player might remark about the man who has just opened a twelve-stitch gash over his left eye. "The boys get in there and like to mix it up a bit. But it's all good fun."

I once asked a friend from Vancouver why hockey players never talk trash about their opponents. He said it was because professional hockey players all started out playing at five o'clock in the morning on ice rinks they'd been driven to by their fathers. The fathers tend to congregate at rink side, watching the boys play. And if the fathers ever hear their sons being abusive, they take them aside and give them an earful, which suggests that you can't learn a whole lot from professional hockey players, but you can learn a lot from their dads. This further suggests that if you want to raise good children, raise them yourselves. Don't wait for the

New York Yankees to teach your kids how to behave, much less the Oakland Raiders. And don't hold your breath waiting for your kids to learn anything useful by watching the World Cup. Baseball, football, boxing, and soccer may be great sports, but they're bad metaphors for virtue.

11: Performance Art

The Faux Creativity of Lady Gaga

Emily Esfahani Smith

IN 2008 LADY GAGA's debut album *The Fame* topped the pop charts worldwide, and its first two singles—the disco-inspired "Just Dance" and sexually provocative "Poker Face"—were international number one hits. In 2009 hungry fans made her the most-Googled female celebrity of the year. In 2010 the sadomasochistic music video for her booming hit "Bad Romance" became the most-watched item in YouTube's history, receiving nearly 180 million views. That same year in March, Yahoo Music reported that Lady Gaga became the only act in the digital era to top the 5 million sales mark with her first two hits, while the tech website Mashable noted that Lady Gaga was the first artist to have her videos reach 1 billion viewer hits. She is the only pop artist in history to earn six consecutive number one hits on the Billboard charts.

How did Lady Gaga become such a standout? To begin with, she's got a knack for sending sadomasochistic rape-like fantasies—in songs and videos that double as catchy club hits—to the top of the charts. The song "Poker Face," which is about being with a man while pretending to be with a woman, alludes to rough sex ("baby when it's love if it's not rough it isn't fun"). The music video for "Bad Romance" is about being a sex slave. The climax of the video occurs when she's thrown at the feet of a group of shirtless, tattooed men who look like Russian mobsters. "I want your revenge," she howls in the song. In the same song, she craves a "leather-studded kiss in the sand." Then there's her song, "I Like It Rough," which needs no explanation.

Lady Gaga is no simple pop star, she is a pop phenomenon—in the overheated rhetoric of the *Atlantic Monthly*, she is "something like the incarnation of Pop stardom itself." Gaga's wild popularity—from the cultlike adoration of her fans, whom she calls "little monsters" (a hat tip to her second album, *The Fame Monster*) to her record-breaking hits—can be chalked up to her creativity, or so say her little monsters. She is "creative and fresh," one young fan tells me, she's "something that I haven't seen before in pop culture." Lady Gaga and her fashion sense are "one and only" in the world, says another, whose first language isn't English. One fan idolizes Gaga's creativity because "she has broken ground and put a new face on this decade of music"—"this decade" being the only one the fan knows culturally.

That new face, in case you've never seen a picture of Lady Gaga, looks like that of a woman posing as a cross-dressing man—a woman who celebrates rough sex, rape-like fantasies, and murder—a woman whose message is, as she told the *Los Angeles Times*, "I want women—and men—to feel empowered by a deeper and more psychotic part of themselves. The part they're always trying desperately to hide. I want that to become something that they cherish." She is all at once vaudevillian and carnal. At all times, she is in full Gaga attire, which means she either looks like a cartoon alien or a "transvestite ballerina," as a writer for the U.K.'s *Times Online* puts it. "Look at her fashion statements," one fan says, when I ask why Gaga is creative.

"I don't look like the other perfect little pop singers," she told *Rolling Stone* in 2009. "I think I look new. I think I'm changing what people think is sexy."

To her young audience, Lady Gaga is the epitome of creativity, which is why she is so successful. But a cursory glance reveals that Lady Gaga is recycling old ideas—and how creative can that be? She takes her cues from Andy Warhol, Queen, Grace Jones,

Prince, and David Bowie. To those with a longer memory than her fans, her disco hits and androgynous flare descend from the glam rock of the 1970s. She is a sexual provocateur, like Madonna was in the '80s and '90s.

Yet her fans swear that she is something new, and different, and rebellious—which is the paradox of creativity in pop culture. In pop culture, the market replenishes itself with new young faces every decade or so. Most of Gaga's fans weren't even alive thirty or even twenty years ago. Here Gaga is cutting edge. "I am fascinated by and respect her uniqueness and unabashed embrace of her own outlandish ideas," one fan swoons.

That definition of creativity has come to dominate the popular culture in modern times—being creative means being novel, outlandish, a one-off. But it was not always thus.

Throughout Western history, the definition of creativity has remained fluid. The concept of creativity was initially limited in the West by strict canons and divine order. Eventually, though, that notion of creativity gave way to a tide of romantic individualism in the nineteenth century and even rebellion in the twentieth century. In the twenty-first century, being a rebellious individual is the apotheosis of creativity.

In the classical Greek world and during medieval times, the concept of creativity was attached to the concept of divinity. Mortimer Adler, the American philosopher who wrote extensively about the West, explains Plato's take: "There are two kinds of creativity—divine and human." Divine creativity "brought the world into being" while human creativity concerns itself, to quote Adler, with the "fashioning of works of art out of natural materials." In making art, humans were not creators, but craftsmen. Art, to Plato, was imitation. He writes that painting "is just the imitation of all the living things of nature with their colors and designs just as they are in nature."

The craftsmen of ancient Greece fashioned their art by following strict canons ordained, they believed, by divine powers. Though the artists were making something new, there was little to no room for imagination, or for creativity as we use the word today. Adler writes, "In the Greek tradition, artistic creativity is associated with discipline, conscious purpose and acquired skill. It is a rational and deliberate process."

For instance, the glowing sculptures of the high classical period in Greek art did not seek to imitate the body of an athlete or a young girl, but they sought to replicate the essence of the platonic form of the body. Keith Sawyer, who has spent his academic career studying creativity at Washington University in St. Louis, notes that the Greek craftsman was "someone who was particularly skilled at representing the pure essences underlying certain forms" using natural materials. And with music, the composers, too, were following a canon: one that replicated the harmony of the orbs in heaven.

The great exception to this rule was poetry. For the Greeks, the poet could be endowed with creativity, but only through communion with the divine—for instance, with the Muses. In this sense, poetic creativity was a form of divine, not human, creativity. Interestingly, in *The Republic*, Plato banished poets from his ideal city, saying that their demonic powers were dangerous.

In the Roman world, the human being became the central focus of art. Rather than depicting the gods or stories from myth in art, as the Greeks did, the Romans focused their attention on emperors and historic events, aristocrats and senators, soldiers and slaves. Art was brought down to earth: humans, not gods, were the subjects of art and the curators of creativity.

But with the onset of Christianity, creation again was delegated to God alone. He created the world from nothing, *creatio ex nihilo*. During the medieval period, artists were viewed as craftspeople—like shoemakers or smiths—hired to serve a function. Patrons would pay artists and specify what they wanted in a work, which was usually religious art for worship. The artist in turn was less an "artist" as we think of the word today—a lone creator—but more of a studio manager. The master and apprentices all worked together to create a work of art. It was not an individual effort.

During the Renaissance, the philosophical ground for individualism was laid. But it took some time for it to be applied in the popular culture. It wasn't until the nineteenth century, with the dawn of romanticism, that creativity became the province of the individual. In that period, the poetic creator, says Sawyer, was a "lone, solitary artist expressing an inner vision."

Think of Samuel Coleridge. He longed to create a public image of himself as a solitary genius. There's a story that he wrote his famous poem "Kubla Khan" in an opium-induced haze—with no revisions. It turns out that Coleridge fabricated this tale. In fact, he labored over multiple drafts of the poem. But he sought a certain image that was admired during that period and still is today (like rock-and-roll singers getting high on drugs and then composing their music—another common fabrication). A few decades later, Sigmund Freud affirmed this notion of creativity. As Adler writes, Freud saw "artistic creativity as originating in the unconscious depths of the mind and as expressive of emotional impulses."

This is the concept of creativity that took hold of Western culture until the mid-twentieth century. Artists like Pablo Picasso and Jackson Pollock even made spectacles of their lone creativity by inviting audiences into their studios to watch them, in their manic crazes, paint. But the 1960s changed all that.

Andy Warhol, the most famous spokesperson of the pop-art movement, rejected the idea of the lone, creative artist. Warhol famously said, "I want to be a machine," "I like boring things," "I like things to be exactly the same over and over again," and "the more you look at the same exact thing, the more the meaning goes away, and the better and emptier you feel." Art was a commodity to be mass-produced for a mass-public, not a carefully planned and executed work that was emotionally inspired—thus Warhol's famous painting of repeating Campbell's soup cans. Authenticity in creativity was out; the market was in.

At the same time creativity was becoming increasingly defined by rebelling against authority and convention. The more provocative one was, the more attention one received and the more successful one could become. Nowhere was deviance more palpable than in the rock-and-roll scene that began in the mid-1950s America and took off in the 1960s. The currency of pop music and pop art was the utter irreverence to authority. With pop music, the best way to inflame social mores was through sex. Think Elvis Presley's hip gyrations. As Camille Paglia, the social critic who wrote *Sexual Personae*, notes, "If you live in rock and roll, as I do, you see the reality of sex, of male lust."

A major point of departure between pop art and pop music, however, was authenticity: bands like the Beatles and the Rolling Stones assumed the image of singer/songwriters, artists who created music themselves. Warhol, by contrast, reveled in inauthenticity. For the next four to five decades in pop music, stars who fashioned themselves as authentic singer/songwriters—like Lou Reed, Bruce Springsteen, and numerous rap stars who allege to be "legit" and from the street—coexisted on the pop-music scene with those who were shamelessly inauthentic—the disco movement, Madonna, and Britney Spears.

In interview after interview, Lady Gaga cites Warhol as a chief inspiration. Like Warhol, Gaga revels in artifice—her songs, videos, and live performances are heavily produced—but she also claims to be authentic, to write her own songs. Like Warhol, she has a manufactured image, which by this point has become an iconic brand, but she's also starkly individualistic.

Lady Gaga's secret may be that she's carefully walked the line between authentic and inauthentic. She has managed to take the market appeal of pop art and the rebellious spirit of rock and roll and combine it with her outlandish individualism. The common thread running through all of these elements of her persona is, of course, sexual deviance and mass-produced hedonism.

A good many pop-culture critics compare Lady Gaga to Madonna, saying that like Madonna Gaga is a savvy exploiter of her sexuality. Madonna, in her 1990 music video, "Justify My Love," was unlike anything seen at the time. The video was banned from MTV for sexual content. She released an entire CD in 1992 called *Erotica*, devoted to sadomasochism. A feature of her world-wide tours was masturbating on stage. By provoking the culture, she ensured that she was a constantly relevant, constantly famous figure in it.

While pushing boundaries is nothing new in the world of pop music, every generation of pop stars must push the boundaries further to make their mark and stay relevant. Lady Gaga knows that to sell more records, especially as a woman, she needs to incorporate sex into her image. And, because she's a savvy busi-nesswoman, she knows that the only way to stay relevant in the market is not just to be sexy, but to do something new with her sexuality that reflects current sexual kinks. In today's culture, homosexual and transgender sexualities are highly fashionable. And to quote a recent Salon.com column by Paglia, "Entertain-ment, media and the arts are nonstop advertisements for homo-sexuality these days." Playing into this, Gaga has adopted an androgynous, homo-sexy look.

Like most people who claim the transgender mantle, Gaga does not look sexy, but grotesque. Instead of pleasure, she celebrates pain. As a *Los Angeles Times* culture columnist writes, "Gaga's work abounds with images of violation and entrapment. In the 1980s, Madonna employed bondage imagery, and it felt sexual. Gaga does it, and it looks like it hurts."

In the age of the Internet, when people have easy and quick access to an ever-larger, ever-replenishing pool of pop music, stars have to do more and more to make themselves stand out against their competition. According to Gary West, a pop-culture expert who has worked in radio, "Her audience likes to see how far she will go. I think that's how they define her creativity."

With Icarian hubris, Gaga thinks she will leave no boundaries behind—and many observers seem to agree: thus, the *Atlantic*'s brash conclusion that "She's the last pop-star: Après Gaga, the void." The real challenge will be creating something from that nothing. Who is up for that?

12: Project Runway
The Surprising Virtues of Style

Herb London and Stacy London

I T IS SOMETHING of a bromide to suggest you can't judge a book by its cover. The presumption in this statement is that appearances can be deceiving. It is true that relying on someone's clothing, exclusively, to determine his or her worth is absurd. But it is equally absurd to argue that style is meaningless. The way the world sees you is important. Whether you acknowledge it or not, your appearance is a statement. It says something about how you *want* to be regarded.

The young woman who wears oversized sweatshirts and Birkenstocks and has unkempt hair may not realize that her look can convey an air of indifference, or conversely, that she does not feel good about herself, that she wants to be invisible. Lady Gaga as an entertainer, on the other hand, intends to shock. Her attire is over the top, flamboyant. She is saying unblushingly, "Notice me."

Indeed, we do ourselves no favors when we pretend that appearances don't matter, even if it seems like a principled stance. A woman I (Herb) am familiar with who graduated from Stanford Law School indicated she was unable to secure a position with a law firm. Looking at her, it was easy to understand why this was the case. She wore combat boots; her tops were at least two sizes too big. She hadn't cut her hair in years and no makeup adorned her face. By my dispassionate standard, she was a mess. With guidance—no, she wasn't a guest on *What Not to Wear*—she learned how to dress and groom herself. She was transformed from Ms. Sloppy into Ms. Professional and, mirablile dictu, she was offered three positions with White Shoe law firms.

Despite the fact there are rules for dressing properly, for example, a man's jacket should be as long as his fingertips and a tie should hit his belt buckle, the key to proper dress is appropriateness. You don't wear a Valentino dress to a rock concert and you don't go to a wedding in shorts.

Some are ignorant of these rules, but some simply flout them as an expression of individualism. Take the issue of "comfort" in clothing. Many people say they will only wear what makes them feel comfortable, even if it is entirely inappropriate. Leaving aside that even the most formal clothing can be comfortable if it fits correctly, this idea of placing comfort above all else is problematic: what you wear, how you manage your own image, tells the world how you want people to treat you. If you dress inappropriately, there is a high probability you won't be treated appropriately or in some cases, even fairly.

In some young people, style is an expression of sexual allure. So often we see young women with extreme décolletage, exposed midriff, or painted-on pants. Modesty may not mean the same thing for a twenty- and a fifty-year-old. Age, body type, situation, and circumstances are factors associated with appropriateness. But it's pretty safe to say: the public should not be seeing "your girls." Put them away. A little bit of décolletage is fine. Leave the rest for your significant other. An open collar is not the same thing as a revealed chest.

Kierkegaard tells the story of a circus troupe traveling the European countryside when one of the clowns notices a fire ripping through the fields driven by fierce winds. Recognizing the danger to a local community, he rides his horse to warn local residents about the impending disaster. But when he gets to the town and explains what is about to happen, no one believes him because he is dressed as a clown.

It is instructive that style is very often associated with legitimacy. We didn't have any idea of Cary Grant's thoughts or opinions, yet we trusted the credibility of his characters on screen, partly due to his tasteful attire. He always looked the part. Being tasteful, of course, doesn't mean that every man should dress like Cary Grant or every woman like Grace Kelly—though, come to think of it, that isn't a bad place to begin.

If clothes convey a message, what should that be? Should fashion call attention to oneself? Should clothing be a manifestation of humility? Fashion, in its best form, is a function of who you are and who you would like to be. (That advice to dress for the job you want not the job you have, is useful.) Some people have a flair for color that suggests something about their personality. Others may prefer subdued shades that reflect a more delicate sensibility.

Beauty matters. *Style* matters. It matters because it exalts the world and endows it with significance. But it also requires discipline. This is clear in *The September Issue,* a documentary about the creation of *Vogue*'s annual fall issue. In the film, cameras follow editor Anna Wintour and creative director Grace Coddington as they spar over the details of what will be the magazine's largest issue. At times the stakes seem small, like when Wintour chastises an editor who picked an accessory the editor thought was "pretty." But at other times, as they wrangle over the location of particular shoots or the details of which photographer would best capture their cover model, the combined work of these two strong-willed women yields beautiful photo spreads that tell engaging stories.

Beauty and discipline can also be found in an exhibition of "Grace Kelly: Style Icon" at London's Victoria and Albert Museum, which shows Princess Grace at various stages of life, with Dior's haute couture skills allowing her to keep a level of gracious glamour even as age intruded on her physical beauty.

Kelly offered a version of fashion as sweet harmony whether she was in the Balenciaga embroidered jacket or slacks for casual wear. One photograph shows her taking her children to school in a Saint Laurent shirt dress that she made into a classic look. She was the embodiment of appropriateness. Whatever her inner circumstance, she illustrated outer evidence of taste.

Contrast that image with a mom of two who wears a skintight Lycra catsuit and stiletto heels to the playground. She may create the wrong impression, even with a great body, even if she's young, even if she is putting a great deal of effort into her style, simply because the outfit is not appropriate to the circumstance. The outfit is shocking in terms of what it says about the person wearing it and may cause incorrect assumptions about that mother's parenting skills. By the same token, the mom who never takes time for herself, who dresses in baggy sweatpants with stains and looks as if she never has time to wash her hair, is also giving off an impression of herself that may not square with her abilities as a parent. Individuals may perceive the women in the examples given here as "unfit" mothers simply because their outward appearance can, sometimes mistakenly, be translated into the virtue of their behavior.

While personal style cannot *define* who an individual is, it should, in the best circumstance, *reflect* who that individual is. What lies at the basis of that reflection has to be a healthy sense of oneself, an understanding of one's place in society, and an acceptance of one's own beauty—one's body as it *is*, not the idealized version of beauty we see on billboards and magazine covers. There is terrific pressure in our society to conform to almost impossible standards of beauty, of thinness, of youth. Those standards have worked against our ability to create our own style; instead they have forced us to be endlessly unhappy with our own uniqueness. And believing in our own accomplishments, being a good mother for example, should in the best-case scenario, directly relate to the style of the woman.

Style is a powerful tool in our arsenal to help us "say" what we want to about who we are and get what we want. If style or image is ignored or mismanaged, the consequences of judgment can be harsh and unfair. At its best, style can help individuals to be recognized for their real achievement and personality.

While Grace Kelly (or Jacqueline Onassis or Audrey Hepburn, for that matter) is often employed as a recognized "standard" of beauty and style, as we may have suggested, we would argue that these women are iconic because their individual styles were appropriate to them. They are examples of women whose style reflected more than just their physical aspects but reflected who they were as people. Grace Kelly dressed her body type well, but she dressed in a way appropriate to a movie star and a princess. We are not all movie stars and royalty.

The key to personal style is self-esteem. But this, too, is a widely misunderstood concept. Some people take self-esteem to mean that you don't care what others think. Or that you don't mind pushing the boundaries of society's rules. One could argue about the underlying psychological issues here, but ultimately self-esteem doesn't necessitate a disregard for others. Even people with a healthy sense of self-esteem understand that they are operating within a certain context. And they don't need to throw all of our social boundaries overboard just to make a point.

Personal style must be based on a larger understanding and appreciation of ourselves as people including our kindness, passion, enthusiasm, curiosity, and so on. In other words, the more we like ourselves, the more we like what we do in the world, our style quite naturally, becomes appropriate to who we are and where we are. It reflects our respect for ourselves as well as for our institutions and our community.

13: Back to Betty Crocker

Why Everyday Cooking Matters

Megan McArdle

SHORTLY AFTER WE got married, it finally happened: the kitchen began encroaching into the living room.

We were renting one of DC's many "flip" houses, the leftovers from the local housing boom. It was one of those more-modern-than-next-week rowhouse renovations where you take a modest Victorian home, remove the interior walls, and turn it into a seamless box. Aside from some maple-veneer cabinetry and tile floors in the kitchen, the entire downstairs was essentially one contiguous space.

It took a while to become familiar with all the home's shortcomings, like the fact that the twin Jacuzzis were fed by a water heater the size of a thimble. But it was obvious even before we moved in that the kitchen Would Not Do. The place seemed to have been expressly designed to tickle the Gracious Living fantasies of . . . well, the kind of people who would rather have a wine refrigerator than another two square feet of counter space.

Seriously. The kitchen came with a wine fridge, and exactly two feet of open counter. Having been raised in a family that does all its Christmas shopping in kitchen outlet stores, I had quite a lot of equipment that I wanted out, where I could use it. There wasn't even room for the KitchenAid stand mixer and food processor, much less the commercial-grade convection oven or the panini press.

But we were desperate. We had been cast back on the housing market during the frozen doldrums between Christmas and the new year because when we showed up at the house we were supposed to be renting it was missing a few things. Like siding. And heat. There was exactly one place on Craigslist that was in both our price range and a neighborhood where we wanted to live. We could have moved into my mother's spare bedroom. We could also have gone hunting for refrigerator boxes, a possibility my husband raised. Twenty minutes after they showed it to us, we were signing a lease.

Thanks mostly to the tireless efforts of my husband, whose profession is journalism, but whose real vocation is Storage, we eventually made it do. We bought kitchen islands and carts from the Internet and created a reasonable approximation of a breakfast bar. Under protest I divested myself of the avocado scoop, the egg poacher, and the fondue pot. By the time we'd been living there for six months, we'd reached a sort of parlous equilibrium—the stuff didn't quite fit into the space we had, but it didn't actually spill out onto the floor either. Until we got married.

The uneasy truce we'd reached with our kitchen equipment was quickly shattered. A salad bowl arrived from a blog reader (thanks, Colin!) which was too big to store without throwing something else out. It lived uneasily atop a counter while we debated which pan we could live without.

But the salad bowl was only an advanced scout. Soon new recruits were pouring into the house daily, and with the cupboards bursting at the seams they quickly spilled over the border between kitchen and living area. The salad bowl moved atop the dining-room shelves and was quickly joined by a half dozen pieces of crockery; an enormous Mauviel roaster wouldn't fit anywhere except under the dining-room table. Before long, a platoon of covered soup bowls had staked out a strategic position on the living-room knickknack shelves. The whole house had been overrun.

Perhaps we could have fought the intrusion a while longer, but the course we settled on was craven capitulation. The day after we returned from our honeymoon, my husband bustled off to Ikea and bustled back with more kitchen shelving. We turned two islands and the wine fridge into a long L that protruded three feet into what had been our dining room. We had to remove one of the leaves from the table and turn it sideways to make everything fit. But when it was all put together, it looked (she said modestly) rather nice.

For the first time in my life, I had what I thought of as a Real Kitchen, the kind where nothing serious could be said to be wanting. I was in a happy daze. In the first two days we were home, I would arise at odd moments from the living-room couch and just sort of wander around our newly transformed kitchen, touching things. Then on the third day—our first day back at work—I came home around 7:30 and began to cook dinner. Specifically, I took two "Cordon Bleu"–style breaded chicken breasts out of the freezer and popped them into the oven at 350 while I dumped prewashed lettuce leaves into our salad bowl, doused them with oil and vinegar, and put it all on the table with some sliced bread.

Which is when the glamour of my new kitchen abruptly wore off. I had all the Shun knives and Le Creuset casseroles a girl could ever want. And just about the time that I acquired them, I seemed to have stopped cooking entirely.

Every generation of my mother's family seems to produce exactly one cook. My great-grandmother Iva's talents were so legendary that the family is still hunting, hopelessly, for the suet pudding recipe that died with her sixty years ago. Yet her daughters ran to Jello molds and cake mixes—except for my grandmother, who remains, to this day, the only person I ever met who could produce a light and flaky pie crust every single time. My aunts rarely even break out a cake mix. My mother, on the other hand, arrived from western New York as a solid basic cook and hurled herself joyfully into New York City's food culture—taking classes with greats like John Clancy and Craig Claiborne and developing a repertoire that extended to things like homemade croissants.

My home revolved around food. Other families went to country homes or played tennis; my family ate. The holiday season began, for us, late in October when my mother would spread the cookbooks and the Thanksgiving issue of *Gourmet* magazine around her on the couch; this was a prelude to a special visit to Oppenheimer's Meats on 98th Street, where my sister and I would gnaw on the slices of bologna that Mr. Oppenheimer gave us while he and my mother debated the merits of various turkeys. Christmas meant, more than gifts, the braided Christmas bread studded with pecans and maraschino cherries . . . and then suddenly it was spring again, and we were shucking new peas at the kitchen table while my mother stirred hollandaise sauce for the artichokes. In the summers we went west to her family and spent long, sticky days making jelly and canning peaches in my grandmother's Formica kitchen. T. S. Eliot's J. Alfred Prufrock measured his life in coffee spoons; I have measured mine in jars of raspberry jam.

This was not some nostalgic idyll of a past where men were real men, women were real women, and cookies came out of the oven instead of the cellophane bag. I grew up in the 1970s and '80s, not the '50s, and for most of my childhood my mother worked outside the home—first as a caterer, and then, when she needed more money for our tuition bills, selling real estate on Manhattan's Upper West Side. My mother cooked because she liked it, and especially because she liked to eat. She didn't have time to cook; she made time to cook. While I was growing up, she did not watch television, and her only other hobbies were mystery novels and the co-op board. The rest of the time that she was not working, she spent in the kitchen. And if we wanted to spend time with her, we spent it chopping.

I am the cook of my generation; my sister's taste runs to starch and plainly roasted meat, and she has mastered exactly two dishes: brownies and Parker House rolls (both of which she makes superbly). I too have the lavish assortment of pots and pans, the shelves full of cookbooks. I make good lasagna, excellent pound cake, and a passable soufflé. I like to cook. I want to cook. I just . . . don't.

All of my lavish kitchenware now reproaches me. It is not just that I am wasting some of the finest comestible technology man has ever designed. It is worse than that. I fear I am becoming the kind of creature that I was raised to despise: what poet Phyllis McGinley once called "the un-cook." The un-cook is not a *non-cook*, which is perfectly honorable. If you don't like to cook, there's no reason to torture yourself, or your family, with your indifferent efforts . . . not when the strip malls are stuffed with decent takeout and the frozen food aisle overflows with passable entrées.

No, the un-cook is someone who has a lavishly appointed kitchen—and tries to spend as little time as possible in it. The kitchen is the culinary equivalent of a Rolex watch—no added utility, just a prop in some fantasy life you'd like other people to think you have.

I have not quite reached the depravity of one host I met, who proudly showed me the fancy kitchen installed that spring, with its gleaming Viking range that had clearly never been used. After all, when I was in my twenties I cooked almost every night. And I still bake cakes for birthdays and housewarmings, marinate chicken skewers and roast potatoes for Sunday dinners, and throw the occasional dinner party. But for myself, and my husband, it is frozen things or food thrown quickly on the grill.

This seems—and is—backwards. There is a reason that so many memoirs center around food; it is one of our most intimate repeated memories. How many memorable dinner parties can you really recall? I can bring to mind a few, of course, like the forty-nine-dish Italian birthday feast I attended a few years ago. But with most people, our true love affair with food begins with the people we love most. They should get our greatest effort, not our least.

I would like to say that I don't have time anymore. I write thousands of words a week, and often work sixty or seventy hours, many of them at very odd times. And my husband is as likely as not to be writing an article in the evening, leaving little time for a leisurely meal and a nice glass of wine. But my mother could have said the same about selling real estate, and she was raising two kids as well. The truth is that I am tired. After a day of trying to be funny, novel, and wise in four blog posts and a column, I cannot muster another spurt of creative energy in the kitchen. I am likely the target audience for popular cooking shows such as Rachael Ray's *30-Minute Meals*, which promise culinary glory in a convenient amount of time. Yet I wait until the weekend dinner parties, when I have a full day to plan, to shop, to think about my food.

I have, as I may have mentioned, a lot of cookbooks. But the one I get the most use out of is not the two-volume *Julia Child*, or the *Gourmet* 800-page omnibus. It is the 1950 *Betty Crocker Picture Cookbook*. My grandmother and my mother each had a copy when I was growing up—well-thumbed, falling apart, splotched with the remnants of long-ago meals. It was the best-selling nonfiction book of its day, and now that it has been reissued, I buy it for every housewarming and bridal shower.

Its appeal is partly its anachronisms, like the section full of hints for housewives that concludes, "If after following all these rules for proper rest, exercise, diet, you are still tired and depressed, have a medical check-up and follow doctor's orders." Why, hello, Valium!

But its style of cookery is still appealing. You need to avert your eyes from its excursions into foreign food, which include some very odd notions about what foreigners might have done with capers and canned tuna. But the heart of the book is simple food, cooked well. It's what cooking looked like when it was still a housewife's main job, which she spent an average of twenty hours a week doing—before vegetable oil was substituted for butter, mixes supplanted baking from scratch, and fast took the place of flavor. The authors are at great pains to provide "economical" dishes that don't use too many eggs and stretch a little meat a long way. It is skilled cooking, but it is not showy. It is just . . . daily.

Contrast that with today's best-selling cookbooks, from celebrity chefs like David Chang, Thomas Keller, and the Barefoot Contessa. The appeal of these books is precisely that ordinary people could not possibly cook like this every day. I recently made Thomas Keller's recipe for fried chicken, which was, as promised, divine—light, crispy, and flavorful. It also took three days to assemble, including an overnight brining step, and two hours to cook. The Barefoot Contessa goes even farther—her television show seems to revolve entirely around throwing an intimate little dinner for some of her wealthy friends. All of this, naturally, takes place in a kitchen somewhat larger than my first New York apartment.

These books sell because that is how we now think about food. You don't cook like this just to eat (we'd get fat); you cook like this to show off. Naturally, to really show off, you need the proper stage setting: gleaming stainless steel and a twenty-three-slot knife block. It's a wonder that my grandmother produced three meals a day for sixty years using the Farberware she picked up at the local hardware store.

I've heard conservatives blame working women for all this, but personally, I blame the men. Over the last fifteen years, as men have gotten more involved in cooking, it's come to seem less like a homely art and more like a contest. The young men I know who cook are mostly interested in ethnic food, made with ingredients acquired in heroic shopping marathons, which they spice to the point where swallowing is an act of physical bravery. They take classes in "knife skills" and vie to see who can acquire the largest cleaver. Not one of them really knows how to bake.

A Catholic I once knew told me that anorexia is as much an act of gluttony as overeating; it elevates food to a wrongful place in your life. For all the tongue-clucking about obesity that you often hear from upper middle-class foodies, I wonder if we middle-class aspirational chefs aren't the worst gluttons of all. When we are alone, we eat almost furtively, slapping the food together as quickly as we can and devouring it alone. And when we are with others, we cannot simply delight in feeding our friends. We must overwhelm them with our food—no, not with our food, but with our marvelous, marvelous selves.

When we moved from that flip house, it took ten hours to pack up the kitchen—more than the rest of the house combined. Now I am contemplating the renovation of the kitchen in the house we just bought—another kitchen that Just Won't Do.

But this time I am thinking of workspace, not places to store all of our stuff. There will be no more gleaming, unused appliances taking up every inch of counter space. I am thinking of the cooking, not the trappings of it. There is virtue in this daily ritual, particularly in an age that values efficiency and speed above all. It is a virtue far removed from the spectacle of the lavishly produced cooking shows or the conspicuous consumption represented by the latest kitchen appliance. It exists in the performance of the ritual itself, a ritual imbued with thoughtfulness and foresight, performed with one's own hands. I certainly hope that, as with my mother and grandmother before me, the kitchen will be the center of our home. But it will only be the center of our lives if there is cooking—everyday, ordinary cooking—actually being done in it.

14: In Search of the Next Great American Songbook

Wilfred M. McClay

A MERICAN CULTURE IS astonishingly dynamic and inventive, always coming up with fresh and unexpected things. Think for example of the amazing outpouring of creative energy, much of it undertaken for the sheer love of it, stimulated by the Internet. And yet American culture also seems to suffer from a guilty reflex. It cannot seem to shake the conviction that it ought to be something other than what it is.

This manifests itself in countless ways. One of them is the view that American culture ought to be producing something it isn't and is instead producing too many things that it shouldn't. The National Endowment for the Arts exhorts that "a great nation deserves great art." But alas, we seem to be the world's high priests of schlock, smut, and throwaway trivia, becoming ever more masterful in producing endless suburban sprawl and pointless gizmos, endlessly multiplying brands of toothpaste and cereal, along with the "creative" advertising that tries to stimulate demands for such products, while in the meantime the great American symphony goes unwritten or unperformed, the great American cities disintegrate, and so on.

That, as I say, is only one view, but it is in many ways the dominant one. Even its seeming opposite turns out on closer inspection to be merely its derivative. From this latter perspective, the source of American culture's failing to meet high standards is our blind acceptance of these obsolete and confining standards themselves, which were after all merely the handmaidens of history's privileged classes. Like Freudian neurotics, we have talked ourselves into feeling guilty for no good reason. The solution is to exorcise the censorious voices, with all their fine distinctions, and then we will be free. Our problem is that we have, in Ralph Waldo Emerson's phrase, "listened too long to the courtly muses of Europe." We need to reject "European" notions of "high culture" and formal excellence and take everything as it comes, cultivating the ability to see beauty and wit wherever there is any expression of vitality—street dancing, vernacular architecture, commercial-strip development, billboards, viral videos, beer cans, landfills . . . even four minutes and thirty-three seconds of silence. We should emulate the inclusiveness of the poet Walt Whitman, the poet laureate of democracy, who declared the scent of his own armpits to be "aroma finer than prayer."

Well, to each his own. This may sound plausible as a gesture in the direction of that most elusive of entities, a truly free and democratic culture. Everything is ultimately of equal worth; everything is equally deserving of our attention and admiration. Then again, the jettisoning of older cultural standards may, for all its pretense of iconoclastic bravado, be nothing more than an implicit confession that American culture couldn't ever possibly measure up to them. Such a fear had been circulating in American society since colonial days. Even so sage a nineteenth-century observer as Alexis de Tocqueville predicted that democracy in America would likely yield little or nothing of distinction in the arts; instead, he averred, the great middle-class commercial republic taking root in North America would be a happy hunting ground for cultural mediocrity. The middling and practical virtues would be cultivated, but not the higher and more disinterested excellences.

Of course, Tocqueville had impeccable theoretical reasons for saying what he did. And of course he proved to be flatly wrong. A decade after the publication of his *Democracy in America*, a great

American literary and cultural efflorescence was in full swing, as writers like Herman Melville and Nathaniel Hawthorne and Edgar Allan Poe and Henry David Thoreau and Emerson and the aromatic Whitman himself (whose poetry was better than his prescriptions) were hitting their stride, impressing not only their fellow Americans but readers around the world.

More generally, the possibility that some of the virtues of American political democracy might have been successfully translated, somehow, into the nation's cultural life has consistently been sold short. But the possibility has never been as far-fetched in practice as it has seemed in theory. In fact, it has happened, and whatever has happened is, by definition, possible. What we have so often lacked is the ability to see what it is that we are already doing, and see it with fresh eyes. That much in the rejectionist critique is true. One might need to look in new places, with an openness to new and unprecedented vehicles, to see genuinely democratic forms of expression emerging, and to learn what such forms have to teach us about living in the world in which we find ourselves.

Which brings me to my subject, the Great American Songbook. This is a term used, loosely and imprecisely, to designate the large group of classic American popular songs first written and performed in the years roughly between 1920 and 1960—roughly, that is, the years between the decline of the sentimental songs of the late Victorian era, and the rise of rock 'n' roll and its various older and younger cousins. The name is slightly misleading, since there is no "book" as such—it's rather like the British constitution in that sense—but there is a remarkable level of agreement as to its contents. It includes the productions of Tin Pan Alley, meaning the New York–based songwriting and music-publishing industry of the day, as well as the Broadway and Hollywood musical theater. It is, let it be noted, an entirely commercial undertaking, dependent for its survival on the favor of the general consuming public, like any other such entertainment business. Far from standing athwart the forces of the market and commerce, it was completely enmeshed in them.

The song titles are still very familiar to most of us: "Night and Day," "All the Things You Are," "Sophisticated Lady," "Stormy Weather," "Stardust," "I Got Rhythm," "My Funny Valentine," "My Favorite Things," "Cheek to Cheek," and "All the Way," just to name a few for starters. So too are the names of the composers and lyricists who produced these songs: respectively, Cole Porter, Jerome Kern, Duke Ellington, Harold Arlen, Hoagy Carmichael, George and Ira Gershwin, Richard Rodgers and Lorenz Hart, Richard Rodgers and Oscar Hammerstein, Irving Berlin, and Jimmy Van Heusen. Jazz musicians and aficionados of jazz are especially knowledgeable about these songs, because they are the "standards" that have formed the core of the jazz repertoire for the past six decades. In fact, it was through my love of jazz that I was led back to an appreciation of the songs themselves, since as a late-end baby boomer, I was far too young to have experienced any of this music in its original form. But after hearing "Stardust" performed for the umpteenth time, I began to wonder where this song had originated.

I can already sense the reader beginning to bristle, thinking that we are heading here for a trip down nostalgia lane, an ode to the lost glories of "the golden age of American song" (as, in fact, this era is sometimes called), a hidebound reactionary's lament about changing tastes, cast in the form of a narrative of general cultural decline. I may not succeed in defeating that suspicion, and I may even be more guilty of the charge than I would like to believe. But I honestly don't think I am, since I don't believe in Spenglerian inevitable cultural decline and instead have great faith in the renewing potential of any culture, and of this one in particular. The point, as students of history know, is that cultures may be renewed most powerfully by the rediscovery of something old. The Italian Renaissance, which was and self-consciously envisioned itself as a movement of recovery, a reappropriation of the wisdom and beauty of the classical world, rather than a radical overthrowing of the Christian order of its day, is a brilliant example of that truth. Similarly, if American culture is to be renewed and revitalized, it will happen not only through the development of new things but also through the revival of old ones and the ethos that went with them.

One should acknowledge the Songbook's limitations. Its contents do not concern great historical events. It makes no pretense to the heroic or epochal, and hardly shows any interest in larger public affairs, or even in public life per se. Instead, the overwhelming majority of the songs are—like most popular music the world over—about romantic love between a man and a woman, with all its excitements, frustrations, mysteries, satisfactions, frustrations, vexations, and ultimate joys. But the lyrics and the music do not attempt to capture love at any and all times. Instead, they capture a particular historical moment, and a particular moral valence, in the evolution of modern relations between men and women.

One of the most creative moments in the life of a culture is the fragile liberalizing moment when the forces of an entrenched and rigid cultural orthodoxy loosen their grip a bit, but not so much as to risk being overwhelmed by disorder. Energies that have been held in check then have their chance to play. That is the moment that these tunes capture. The songs are urbane, witty, playful, intelligent, occasionally naughty (in an oblique way), but also full of heart and spirit, neither brutally sexual nor relentlessly high-minded, but ultimately (in the aggregate) altar-directed and commitment-affirming. There still is courtship, there still are rules, but there also is a kind of easygoing freedom, within well-understood limits. They perfectly express the interlude between the loosening of strict nineteenth-century mores and the onslaught of the post–World War II cultural revolution. The ethos of the songs is post-Victorian but pre–no fault divorce, not to say pre-hookup culture. Even the racier lyrics of Cole Porter (see, for example, the Noah's

Ark list of the animals that "do it" in "Let's Fall in Love") have a lightness and humor to them, and a sense of their own edginess, that makes them fit their moment.

What is remarkable to our ears today is the easy combination of an unabashed romanticism about love ("I'm gonna love you, like nobody's loved you / Come rain or come shine"—Johnny Mercer/ Harold Arlen) in such close relationship with an urbanity, verbal ingenuity, and playfulness that one would more usually associate with skeptical distancing ("Love is like the colic or the measles: / Almost ev'rybody gets it once"—Dorothy Fields). Occasionally the two mentalities are even brought together brilliantly, as in this snatch from the chorus of Porter's "It's All Right with Me": "You can't know how happy I am that we met, / I'm strangely attracted to you. / There's someone I'm trying so hard to forget, / Don't you want to forget someone too?"—a sentiment that should strike a chord with anyone who has ever been on the rebound.

But the brilliance of the songs is in their playful but perfect marriage of their words and their music. So one must also pay homage to the formal musical qualities of the Songbook's contents, which perfectly suited it to carry such lyrical freight. The form was, in a sense, simplicity itself. Many of the songs, especially those originating in musicals, contain an introduction, called the verse, which is designed to make the transition from dramatic action to the action-suspension of the song, but these introductions have over the years generally been dropped, as the songs have come to stand independently of the shows they were originally part of. What is left is a very standard but supple structure, a thirty-two-bar chorus immediately graspable by listeners, but susceptible of all manner of melodic and harmonic innovation. That combination of order and openness made a wonderfully adaptable vehicle for popular song, capable of accommodating everything from the simplest jingle to the lush and complex harmonies of a song like Jerome Kern's "All the Things You Are." And the melodies are always marvelously memorable and eminently singable, something that surely can't be said of more than a fraction of the popular music since 1960.

The Songbook's contents perfectly illustrate the familiar principle that art needs the freeing discipline of limits in order to flourish. Not too many limits, and not overly constraining ones, but the right kind of limits—sturdy, adaptable, unfussy. And the requirement to be entertaining, for one of the key limits placed on the Songbook writers is that their music had to sell, and so had to have general appeal. It could not be precious or abstruse, or preachy, or self-involved. An important part of its artistry was to wear its art lightly, even with a little self-deprecation. The discipline imposed by the popular market was an essential part of what made the Songbook great and so deeply expressive of a modern democratic culture. It was a limit that produced a flourishing form.

And as the form flourished it gave expression to an ethos, one to which I think we can profitably return—not to wallow in it nostalgically, or readopt it anachronistically, but to learn something from it about the art of living. Not only about how men and women might order their lives together with great civility, seriousness, refinement, playfulness, and yes, love. But also about the expressive potentialities of a more genuinely democratic art. For the Songbook is an expression of what is possible in American culture, in its blending of high and low, its intelligence and wit, its beauty and ingenuity, its sheer pleasure and accessibility, and the incomparable palette of many colors that its lyrics bring to our understanding and appreciation of the endlessly fascinating phenomena of romantic love. And like all great works of art, it forms us as we listen to it, shapes our expectations, cultivates us, cultures us. It explains our perplexities in love and makes merry with them at the same time. If the Songbook teaches us about art flourishing within limits, it might be said with equal justice that its songs teach the same lesson about love. Not too many limits, and not overly constraining ones, but limits nonetheless.

The history of ideas and emotions is tracked in the history of words; and popular music tracks a word like "love" exceedingly well. Something happened to that word in the thirty years between "Our Love Is Here to Stay" (1937), the last of the great Gershwin brothers' songs, to the Doors' "Love Me Two Times (I'm Goin' Away)" (1967), just as something had happened in the years between Stephen Foster's genteel and immaterial love songs (his "Jeanie with the light brown hair" was "Borne, like a vapor, on the summer air") or Jean Lefarve's 1919 "Dear Heart" ("Dear heart, are you true to me, My heart yearns for only thee") and the more fully embodied, more playful, occasionally carnal, and yet no less idealistic and heartfelt expressions of love to be found in the contents of the Songbook. If the sentimentality of the old regime was awful in its own way, the opposite extreme as we have experienced it since the sixties has been awful in its. The ethos of the Songbook years look immensely appealing in comparison to either one.

And yet, one realizes with a start that the Doors' song, which uses the word "love" to signify something that is, whatever its virtues, rather distinct from love, is now forty-five years old. What does this mean? It means that, for all of the creativity and dynamism that I described at the outset of this essay, we are in other respects in the grip of a cultural orthodoxy, one that is all the more pernicious for its being unacknowledged as one, even by itself.

To make it more vivid, consider this. For a young person in 1967, the act of thinking one's way back forty-five years into the past meant taking oneself back to 1922, to the presidency of Warren G. Harding—that is, to a time that felt, in 1967, very nearly as distant and ancient as it would today. And yet, by way of contrast, I can rely for certain on the fact that nearly all of my undergraduate students will know exactly who the Doors were, will know the lyrics to their songs, and the lyrics to an astonishing number of

popular songs that were already considered to be venerable clas-
sics when I was in college in the 1970s.

This is astonishing. And sad. They deserve something better.
In the Great American Songbook they have a place to begin their
search.

Part 4

Building a Better You

15: Controlling Our Bodies, Controlling Ourselves

Daniel Akst

I F JOHN BUNYAN were alive today but still infused with religious passion, how might he get his message across? Surely not by writing a book-length allegory like *The Pilgrim's Progress.*

No, nowadays a Puritan prophet might likelier blog and perhaps gather up a few thousand Twitter followers. But these are mostly tools for niche audiences. Bunyan wrote for the masses. *The Pilgrim's Progress,* when it was published in 1678, was not considered an esoteric religious tract but a work of popular literature. It soon proved a runaway best seller embraced by readers of every social class.

Given this orientation, Bunyan today would probably take his message to TV. And the program he would create, if it didn't already exist, might be *The Biggest Loser,* the granddaddy of a thriving genre of weight-loss reality shows that has included *Big Medicine* (about bariatric surgery), *One Big Happy Family* (in which the whole clan slims down together), and *Dance Your Ass Off,* about which the less said the better.

Think of these shows as modern-day allegories of self-transformation, ones that speak to our culture as compellingly as *The Pilgrim's Progress* spoke to that of our forebears. Being on *The Biggest Loser*—or striving to lose a lot of weight under any circumstances—really is a kind of pilgrimage, one beset by the usual hazards of temptation, weakness, and doubt. It's a journey one makes in the direction of self-mastery through a hostile landscape studded with fast food and malevolent co-workers bearing baked goods.

These shows tell us a lot about ourselves. The message at first is predictably grim: we are a crass and exhibitionistic people, glutted by excess and devoted to voyeurism, if not schadenfreude. Often these programs, like so much TV, are maudlin and, frankly, exploitative. Yet ultimately I came to think that the folks who appear on these shows are worthy of our admiration for doing so—and that the people who create them understand quite a lot about human nature.

What these shows demonstrate is that willpower is weak and without practical wisdom unlikely to triumph. We are likely to have more success, to cite one relevant example, keeping ice cream out of the house than resisting its siren call from the freezer. The good news is that even the weak of will have opportunities to constrain their own choices, if only they acknowledge their weakness and take up arms against it. As Rousseau says in *The Confessions,* "If we chose always to be wise, we should rarely need to be virtuous."

At the same time, these shows vividly dramatize the challenge of moderation—that virtue of virtues—in a world of freedom and affluence. They are cautionary tales about the ways in which we can fall short of our own fondest wishes for ourselves by succumbing to powerful lesser desires on a daily basis. Each indulgence of these appetites is insignificant in itself—what's one bite?—but taken together they can impose a burden heavy enough to warp our lives.

Of all the fat shows, *The Biggest Loser* is the closest to a cultural phenomenon (it averaged around ten million viewers in 2010), and it remains the purest example of the genre. Basically, each season a group of fat people is selected to compete in a contest to see who can lose the most weight. This project involves considerable suffering on treadmills and the like, to say nothing of caloric deprivation. Although the contestants are shown in their homes, sometimes in exaggerated poses of consumption, much of the action takes place at a retreat where the contestants are subject to verbal flagellation—for their own good, of course—at the hands of painfully thin conductors on the rocky road to fitness.

As you might guess from this summary, *The Biggest Loser* is also the show that hews most closely to *The Pilgrim's Progress.* For *Biggest Loser* contestants, being selected for the program is a dream come true—one much like the narrator's dream of Christian and his spiritual pilgrimage in Bunyan's book. The contestants, most of them so heavy they seem beyond hope of redemption, have a great weight that they're looking to shed, just as Bunyan's Everyman hero is trying to do with the weight strapped to his back.

In both sagas the burden appears to be the weight of sin, except in this case it's the sin of overindulgence. Yet whether you believe in original sin or just the virtue of self-mastery, at some level all sinning, ancient and modern, is about the control of desire, and in this sense *The Biggest Loser* is a morality tale just as Bunyan's was. Contestants who desperately want to behave differently are defeated by their own uncontrollable appetites, a position in which almost all of us find ourselves sooner or later. "I do not do what I would like to do," Paul lamented in his letter to the Romans, "but instead I do what I hate . . . so I am not really the one who does this thing; rather it is the sin that lives in me."

Having failed to regulate their desires, *Biggest Loser* contestants embark on the show's journey as fallen, and this profound spiritual infirmity is visible to all in their great unhideable girth, which broadcasts their shame as clearly as if they wore a scarlet letter. Their goal on the program is to put down that weight, unburden themselves of their sin, and number themselves among the elect—the minority of American adults whose body weight is in the range of normal.

All this is to say that *Biggest Loser* contestants have already been through Bunyan's Valley of Humiliation by the time they are on the show, and with their health troubles linger dangerously in the Valley of the Shadow of Death, as the show's appalled doctor dramatizes for us. But the powerful premise of this series is that America's fatties have the power to change. Like Bunyan's pilgrim, they can choose salvation. The difference is that self-discipline, rather than Jesus, is held to be the answer. This is America, after all, where each of us is supposed to be our own savior.

Yet *Biggest Loser* participants know they can't do it alone. None of us can, which may be why contestants tearfully embrace the show's glamorous trainers—hard-body messiahs who hold out the prospect of redemption through suffering. (*Biggest Loser* seasons often focus on couples or even whole families, as if to underscore the group nature of our failings.) The painful exercises the show's trainers demand offer a way for their overweight charges to atone for the pleasures of overeating, a form of self-abuse that participants have evidently indulged in for years, at least judging by the evidence of their massive bodies, which betray their past as effectively as the rings of a tree trunk disclose its age.

Virtue, it seems, requires struggle, for dieters as much as for Bunyan's pilgrim, and in both cases it's a life-and-death conflict. Indeed, redemption for *Biggest Loser* contestants can occur only if they are reborn in a different body. Contestants testify that they haven't had a boyfriend or girlfriend, that they are the life of the party who inevitably goes home alone, that they dream of the love and happiness that will one day be theirs if only they can slim down. Their goal, in other words, isn't just weight loss but a new life in a version of heaven—a heaven of normality—that they can only reach by emerging from the chrysalis of the program's retreat resurrected as their own masters.

The desire to attain the promised land of thinness—and a recognition that, on their own, they are powerless in the face of their appetites—goes a long way toward explaining why people sign up for these programs. Sartre's famous comment notwithstanding, hell is not other people. On the contrary, social ties are crucial for establishing and enforcing norms—and helping each of us defer gratification and resist unseemly excess.

Those ties have become frayed in modern society. In some cases, as when an entire family or neighborhood is overweight, communal ties reinforce harmful norms. On *The Biggest Loser*, the audience performs the norming function that tight-knit communities once did, applying social pressure, moral support, and a sense that for better or worse somebody is watching. This is how a great deal of human behavior is moderated.

"Our friends and relatives," the psychologist Howard Rachlin writes, "are essential mirrors of the patterns of our behavior over long periods—mirrors of our souls. They are the magic 'mirrors on the wall' who can tell us whether this drink, this cigarette, this ice-cream sundae, this line of cocaine, is more likely to be part of a new future or an old past. We dispense with these individuals at a terrible risk to our self-control."

By committing to their quest so publicly, participants on these shows make it much more difficult for themselves to give up. John Norcross, a psychologist at the University of Scranton, has studied New Year's resolutions and found that making a public commitment is a good way to increase the odds of living up to them. Faced with the prospect of embarrassment, you'll work that much harder to stick to the resolutions you've proclaimed to be your own. Failure, as Ed Harris said in *Apollo 13*, is not an option.

To the extent *The Biggest Loser* serves as a powerful commitment device for people who need help in this department, it does so in a rich tradition much older than *The Pilgrim's Progress*. Demosthenes is said to have embarrassed himself into seclusion for three months by intentionally shaving half his head. Unwilling to be seen in public until it grew back, he used the time to work on his rhetorical skills. In an Internet version of the same scheme, the sociologist Jeffrey J. Sallaz at the University of Arizona overcame procrastination by posting an embarrassing picture of himself on Facebook, which he resolved to leave there until he finished reviewing copyedits on a manuscript he'd produced.

Self-embarrassment can be effective, but dieters have relied on other poison-pill techniques as well. In a book called *The Black-mail Diet*, author John Bear suggested people could force themselves to lose weight by committing to some hideous consequence if they didn't. Bear himself slimmed down by pledging to donate $5,000 to the American Nazi Party if he failed. He didn't.

The Internet is bringing such enterprising self-management techniques to the masses. A website called Stickk.com enables users to enter legally binding agreements to lose weight or accomplish practically any other goal on pain of financial penalty. When you make a commitment on Stickk.com, have your credit card ready. If you fail in your contractual quest, your money goes to the designated charity of your choice—or perhaps more motivating still, to the anticharity you choose, along the lines that John Bear evidently pioneered. Stickk.com's motto: "Put out a contract on yourself."

But giving individuals the tools to commit to virtue isn't the same as establishing a social climate that uses the power of inertia to make virtuous action into a kind of default. Today's hypercaloric environment, in which family meals have disintegrated, portion sizes have exploded, and snacks are ubiquitous, has made fat into something like a national norm. More than two-thirds of Americans are overweight and about half of those are obese, numbers that suggest a truly massive public health problem. Estimates of the health impact vary, but one reasonably good one, from a 2009 study (*The Preventable Causes of Death in the United States*) by leading scientists in the field, found that if we could get everybody in America to slim down to an appropriate body weight, we'd prevent 216,000 premature deaths annually.

Few of those lives will be saved by means of a painful personal pilgrimage like the ones portrayed on *The Biggest Loser*. Instead it will require cultural and political changes that make us more active and less susceptible to our own unruly appetites. We'll need to help one another to form better habits, and perhaps better priorities as well. In short, we will have to come together in some way, at the very least for meals, but probably for policy changes as well. Virtue, in this arena as in so many, is a collective activity, and the revolution in our behavior, when it comes, is unlikely to be televised.

16: Public Broadcasting

The Allure of Overexposure

Rob Long

NOT LONG AGO, I was enjoying an episode of Bravo TV's repellent, grotesque, and thoroughly addictive *Real House-wives of New York City.*

(Please stay with me here. I could waste time claiming merely to have been "flipping around" the dial; I could say that it "was on in an airport lounge"; I could even blame, outlandishly, some kind of "TiVo malfunction." But the truth is, I was watching it, at home, by choice. Don't judge me.)

Real Housewives of New York City, for those who aren't famil-iar, is a reality television program that follows the exploits of self-described "society women" in the Big Apple. Each episode records in garish detail their petty squabbles and minor triumphs—the whole awful tacky tapestry of their deeply middle-class lives, the striving and social climbing and backstabbing, the shrieking hissy fits and unhinged behavior. The entire series—and its sisters, *The Real Housewives of Orange County, Atlanta, New Jersey,* and now *Washington, DC*—emits such a nasty, sulfurous pong and displays behavior so offensive and sociopathic that it's a mystery to me why it's not an even bigger hit.

One of the housewives, though, wasn't really a housewife at all: she was a single career gal when the episode was shot—I think her tagline in the credits is something like "New York City is my playground"—but at the time, she was in a relationship with a guy whom she described as shy and reserved.

When he appeared on camera, however, he didn't seem shy or reserved, he just seemed like a guy who didn't really want to appear on camera in a reality TV show. He seemed like a guy who was dating a woman who announced to him one day that she had been asked by some producers from Bravo TV to do a show called *The Real Housewives of New York City*, and instead of saying, like a reasonable person, "Are you out of *your mind*?" said, instead, "Sure! When can we start rolling?"

In every scene he's in, he keeps avoiding the lens, keeps ducking behind stuff. He seems painfully aware that there are several cameras whirring around him, a boom mike pointed at his face, and that everything he says, does, or mumbles is going to be blasted on television for millions of people to watch (and then lie about watching).

In other words, he seems perfectly well adjusted, which when edited properly by television professionals comes across as sullen and uncommunicative.

So in the episode of *The Real Housewives of New York City* that I saw, the nonhousewife sits her shy boyfriend down for a Serious Talk about Where This Relationship Is Going, which she's prepared herself for—unbeknownst to him but beknownst to the viewer—by drinking seven martinis.

It's a very sloppy ambush.

"Don't you think it's time we moved in together?" she slurs. "Can we talk about where this relationship is going?" she asks, with the kind of elaborate composure only drunks can manage.

His eyes dart around to the cameras and the microphones and he says the only smart thing I've ever heard anyone on a reality TV show ever say.

He says, "Can we talk about this later?"

"You don't want to talk about this *now*?" she pleads.

"Can we talk about this later?" he repeats, as we watch him slowly, surely, fall deeply out of love with her.

And I think, after that, they break up or something—I'm not really sure because of course I never watch that kind of trash. But I loved that phrase.

"Can we talk about this later?"

Meaning, when the cameras aren't on. Meaning, when every word and gesture isn't getting recorded and saved for some editor to clip and some music supervisor to score and some promo guy to cut and use seventeen times. And if everyone—or at least *one* person—on every reality show—or at least on *some* reality shows —said those words—"Can we talk about this later?"—then reality television might not be so lurid and exhibitionist and creepy.

In other words, not so interesting.

Reality television stars always say the same thing when they're asked about it later. I'm not that awful, they claim, I'm just edited that way. The producers *wanted* me to pitch a fit/betray a friend/ drink too much/create that scene. It's *television*, they all say, when confronted on *Oprah* or Bravo TV's own *Reunion* series, in which feuding reality stars hit the sofa for more fireworks. Don't hate us, they say. We're just performers. In reality, we're not so interesting. On reality television, though, we're compulsively watchable.

Perhaps, more than all the bad behavior and the nasty words— more than Snooki—that has been reality television's most significant cultural contribution. We seem no longer satisfied with living our day-to-day lives. We want always to be watchable.

Of course, the reality stars have editors. For years, the Writers Guild of America has claimed that the story editors—those sad souls tasked with watching endless footage and cutting it all down into hour-long powerplays of nastiness and psychosis—aren't just editors, but *writers*, and as such covered by the basic agreement between the Guild and the studios. They shape unformed mate- rial into a story, says the Guild, and that's what writers do. And the material, in turn, is shaped by on-set producers who goad and prod their subjects into being just a little more angry, just a little more crazy, just a little more . . . interesting.

The result is a creepy kind of feedback loop: the story editors try to identify and shape emerging story lines, which they relay back to the on-set producers, who manipulate their subjects into delivering satisfying moments of television based on those emerging story lines—big end-of-show blowups, promotable snippets of suspense—so that what is billed as "reality" is, in fact, carefully plotted, by everyone involved.

Reality television stars are in on this, too. I was just trying to give the producers what they wanted, they all say. My job was to be interesting, outlandish. "I know why I'm here," one of the housewives said on one of the *Housewives* shows. "I'm supposed to be the crazy one."

And we, of course, can tsk-tsk all we want. But in many ways we're all living to be watched.

I have a friend who updates his Facebook status several times a day. Sometimes his updates are innocuous—"enjoying the new Ryan Adams CD" or "loving my chicken Caesar wrap"—but often they're more complicated, mentioning certain restaurants, chic venues, glamorous locations. "Drinks at Chateau Marmont, then dinner at Lucques! I'm loving LA in April"—things like that.

In one amazing twenty-four-hour span, his Facebook updates reported a power breakfast ("Omelets at Geoffrey's in Malibu with my agent!") and a business lunch ("Chipotle burritos with writing staff to work out this season's story lines") and a romantic end of day ("Grateful for Michelle and a beach sunset at the end of a busy day"), absolutely *none of which* was true, because on that day I happened to run into him at the E-Z Lube near my house, in shorts and a dirty T-shirt, getting his oil pump replaced, which was a four-hour job.

I confronted him about this later. "I've done all of those things," he insisted. "Just not in one day."

"But that's lying," I said. "You're lying on Facebook!" I'm not sure, in retrospect, why I thought this was such a big deal. He certainly didn't.

He looked at me strangely. "So?" he asked.

"So," I said, "Facebook is supposed to be true. It's supposed to be factual."

"Oh," he said, leaning back smugly. "So you really 'like' everything you 'Like' on Facebook?"

"Well . . . ," I muttered.

"And you're really 'friends' with all of your Facebook Friends?"

He had me there.

"Stop thinking of Facebook as something real," he said. "It's not. It's just . . ." And here he paused for a moment, searching for the right word. "It's just . . . content," he said. "That's all. Just content."

He shrugged. "I'm a Hollywood writer," he said. "I'm just delivering what people want to think a Hollywood writer does all day. I'm just giving people something interesting to read."

He's just providing content, in other words, like one of the Real Housewives. He's doing what he thinks he's supposed to do, in the reality television series called "Facebook."

And it's not just Facebook. The same thing happens on Internet services like Twitter—on which hundreds of millions of people worldwide announce their tiny insights to each other, in bursts of no more than 141 characters—and the rapidly growing Foursquare, a mobile phone application on which people broadcast their exact location, earn points and "badges" for being in a lot of cool places, and in general provide a narrative in which our deepest, most neurotic suspicion that all of our friends are doing more interesting things and having more interesting lives is utterly confirmed.

And if Twitter and Foursquare aren't your thing, there's Plurk, Gowalla, or StickyBits, all of which will tell random strangers what you're thinking, what you're doing, and where you are. (Oh, and it'll tell advertisers, too.)

Phenomenally popular sites like Yelp.com allow users to review restaurants, merchants, outdoor venues—anything, really, that can be rated and discussed has a Yelp entry, complete with long, personal narratives ("My girlfriend and I were in the mood for great Chinese food . . .") and lots of identity creation ("As you Yelpers know, I'm pretty much Old School when it comes to bike shops. So imagine my surprise when . . ."). Add Yelp together with Foursquare, and you can critique your day in real time. Channel all of those updates and reviews into Facebook—it's easy to do; all of those services offer that option—and you can cyber-cobble an identity almost as irritating and narcissistic as a Real Housewife.

Text too restrictive? Try video. You can become a star on You-Tube—one of the fastest growing categories of videos is the "vlog," in which people just talk into the camera. Or go live at Ustream .tv (or Justin.tv or Kyte.tv . . .).

Thanks to an environment of near-unlimited bandwidth, we may not need stars anymore. We're all busily creating content for each other, living up to (or down to, depending) our reputations. Or, sometimes, creating them out of whole cloth while we spend the day at the E-Z Lube.

And we're doing it for much the same reason that the Real Housewives do it. We're doing it because people are watching—either on Bravo or YouTube or Facebook or Twitter. We're doing it because there's a content vacuum that wants to be filled. We're doing it because all of these tools allows us to be stars. They may call it "social networking," but that doesn't make it "social." Social networks are All About Me.

Still, a lot of people, like the Real Housewife's Boyfriend who insisted on "talking about this later," are uncomfortable with all of this self-broadcasting. If you type "How Do I . . ." into Google, its auto-fill feature will return ". . . delete my Facebook account" in the top ten suggestions. So, clearly, lots of people want to know how to turn these systems off.

Yet nothing has slowed the growth of these services. Facebook has over four hundred million active users. In 2007 Twitter served up about five thousand Tweets per day. In early 2010 that number was fifty *million*. And reality television franchises like *The Real Housewives of...* continue to grow. The A&E cable network has a series called *Intervention* (about drug abusers), one called *Hoarders* (compulsive pack rats), and an even more bleakly titled show, *The Incurables* (people who are just plain nuts). A&E has streamlined the process: they don't need to goad a Real Housewife into acting crazy; they just hire a crazy one in the first place.

So when the Real Housewife's boyfriend squirmed uncomfortably in front of the camera, he was displaying something increasingly rare.

Shame. Embarrassment. An awareness that one's public face was something worth protecting, worth holding back. A sense that there's something dirty about creating "content" for other people out of your own life. That, ultimately, it's more important to *have* character than to *be* a character.

Of course she broke up with him.

17: Lessons for Life
The Virtues of Continuing Education

Patrick Allitt

AMERICANS WERE enthusiastic about education right from the beginning. The first generation of Puritan settlers had scarcely gathered a couple of harvests and caught a few fish before they began setting up Harvard College in 1636, "dreading to leave an illiterate ministry to the churches when our present ministers shall lie in the dust." By the time of the American Revolution more than half of the white men and women in the colonies could read. Early in the nineteenth century Horace Mann, secretary of the Massachusetts Board of Education, set to work creating what is now the public school system. Mann and his heirs conceived the daring idea of universal literacy and numeracy; they were the direct ancestors of "No Child Left Behind."

It's always been a struggle trying to educate everyone. Children in the nineteenth century, like children today, showed widely differing degrees of aptitude and enthusiasm—some of them *wanted* to be left behind. A nation with such a generous immigration policy, moreover, was taking in hundreds of thousands of adults who had had little or no schooling in their lands of origin. They needed access to adult education. The nation responded vigorously, setting up a wide array of "Americanization" programs in the late nineteenth and early twentieth centuries. Men and women of every age who attended these programs, starting new lives in the New World, learned not only how to say phrases like "George

Washington was the father of his country" and "I am an American" but to *write* them, too.

Learning doesn't get easier as you get older. Children acquire
languages with astonishing speed and facility whereas adults
struggle; anyone who begins English after age twenty is unlikely
ever to speak it without a strong accent. Most other subjects come
easiest to youngsters, too. On the other hand, grown-ups have a
keener appreciation of why education matters. Those who lack it
understand what they are missing and even those who *have* had
the chance early in life haven't always made the best use of their
opportunities.

All the industrial democracies today hold out opportunities for
lifelong learning but none has such a massive educational infra-
structure for all age groups as the United States, nor such ease
of access. Most states are barred from discriminating by age in
their college admissions policies (such discrimination is common
in Europe), and the colleges are complemented by an array of vol-
untary, church-oriented, and for-profit educational opportunities
catering to just about every need. As the life expectancy of Americans increases, and as ever-larger numbers enjoy better health for
longer, the market for education keeps on growing.

Why do people want to learn? Part of the answer is vocational—
they understand that the ability to read, write, compute, analyze,
and interpret will improve their ability to get and hold good jobs.
There's more to it than that, however. We all take pleasure in
things beyond the purely functional and utilitarian. Aspects of the
world around us catch our fancy; we scrutinize them and realize
how complicated they are, and then we begin to read about them,
or take classes about them, confident that increasing our knowledge will increase our appreciation and enjoyment. The nature of
most people's work requires them to develop a few skills to a high
pitch while neglecting many others. Millions respond by using
their leisure time and discretionary income in developing other
areas of their lives and minds.

As a college history professor I regularly get requests to speak to adult groups of all kinds. Whenever possible I say yes, partly because it often pays but mostly because I believe it's the right thing to do. It's gratifying work too since, as a rule, learners become more grateful as they get older. College undergraduates are lovely people but they rarely thank me for teaching their classes; to them college is the automatic next step along the road to their careers rather than something they chose. Older students, by contrast, have *decided* to learn. They shower me with thanks and it's hard not to bask in their praise.

Regularly, here in Atlanta and at sites around the country, I give workshops for groups of middle school, high school, and college-level teachers. Sometimes these are pedagogy workshops, in which I try to pass along insights I learned during a long stint as director of Emory's Center for Teaching and Curriculum. More often they are "content enrichment" seminars, designed to help history teachers learn more history and care about it more. Chances are the participants were education majors in college and learned more about educational psychology and classroom management than they did about Pickett's Charge and the Treaty of Versailles.

Lifelong learning isn't just a matter of professional enrichment, however. For each of the last fifteen years I've also been the teacher to a group of thirty-five history enthusiasts, many of them senior citizens, in Atlanta. It is called the Habersham Group because most of its members live on or near to Habersham Road in Buckhead. Twelve times each year, on the second and fourth Monday of every month between September and April (except for a Christmas break in December) we have a two-hour class. Members take turns to be hosts. I arrive at the chosen home at 7:30 and speak for an hour, after which there is a thirty-minute break for chat, snacks, and wine, followed by another half hour of discussion and questions. I choose a new theme each year, usually one related to my current research and writing, and divide it into twelve manageable units.

Among the many pleasures of teaching the group is exploring the members' long memories. Episodes in twentieth-century history are not, to them, simply the stuff of textbook prose. Many of them *remember* what it was like to live through the Second World War, the civil rights movement, and the upheavals of the Vietnam era. When I first joined the group one of the oldest members, a man in his nineties, was a veteran of the pre–World War II Flying Tigers who fought in the Chinese war against Japan. Another had landed at D-Day, a third had sailed on convoy escorts through the submarine-infested North Atlantic, while one of the women had worked for J. Edgar Hoover in the pioneering early days of the FBI. Unlike my undergraduates, they have plenty to say about their experiences, like to challenge me on points of detail, and often add fascinating and relevant stories from their own lives.

Their motive is strictly education for its own sake rather than education for vocation or for certification. They have embraced fully an ideal that we try hard, not always successfully, to urge on young people, that of the liberal arts. Most of America's best colleges pride themselves on liberal arts education, requiring students to study some history, some literature, a foreign language or two, a science, a social science, and some mathematics. This curriculum, according to college catalogues and campus tour guides, will make them well-rounded citizens and nurture in them a lifelong appreciation for the finer things in life and the intricate complexity of civilization. In reality large numbers of students resent having to take courses that have no bearing on their intended careers and that seem almost defiantly impractical. They stump around campus saying: "I've *got* to take a math class," or "I still haven't done my language requirement," in tones more grumpy than liberated. Retirees take the opposite view: the liberal arts are just what they want after lifetimes of hard practical work in specialized and often monotonous fields of labor. The supposed irrelevance of courses on Greek drama, classical architecture, comparative religion, and cosmology is what now makes them so alluring.

Part of the craving for lifelong learning comes from the decline of what used to be two great sources of intellectual nourishment: politics and preaching. In the nineteenth century politicians were expected to be first-rate orators; audiences would flock to listen to the best of them. Before the Civil War Daniel Webster and Edward Everett could bring tears to their audiences' eyes as they evoked the memory of George Washington and the heroism of the Sons of Liberty. They could also arouse furious resentment against "King" Andrew Jackson during the Bank War of the 1830s. Seventy years later William Jennings Bryan and Theodore Roosevelt were spellbinders, too, immensely entertaining as well as immensely learned, whose booming speeches (unaided by microphones and loudspeakers) sometimes lasted for hours and captivated huge audiences. The art of political speech making went into decline in the mid- and late twentieth century, displaced by the needs of television for short sound bytes. Is there anyone today who is famous in America principally as an orator? I don't think so.

The quality of preaching deteriorated along with the quality of political speech making. Students today often learn with dismay that church sermons used to be two or three hours long. They're dismayed because they equate sermons with boredom. What they don't learn is that eighteenth- and nineteenth-century congregations were often delighted by long sermons because of their extraordinary high quality. The ministers were the most highly educated people in town, men of great prestige and learning, accomplished in oratory, untroubled by rivals like radio and TV, and brimming with faith and conviction. George Whitefield, Charles Grandison Finney, Dwight Moody, and many others were long, long talkers, but we don't have evidence to suggest that their audiences wanted them to finish sooner. Today's clergy, by comparison, are (with a few honorable exceptions) far less distinguished intellectually and have become estranged from the rich rhetorical tradition that sustained their predecessors. No wonder the kids get restless in their pews after ten minutes of today's feeble sermonizing. As the quality of political and religious rhetoric declined, the human thirst for learning, and learning as a form of entertainment, had to turn to other sources.

In addition to my work with teachers and senior citizens I am also involved in a project that reaches thousands of learners I never actually meet. This is The Teaching Company (TTC), founded in 1990 and now well known nationwide. Its founder, Tom Rollins, a Harvard Law School graduate, was working as chief counsel to a Senate committee when he conceived the idea. He speculated that thousands of adult professionals, like him, would probably enjoy college-level courses in a wide array of disciplines, that they would be willing to pay for the experience, and that they would welcome the chance of learning for its own sake, with no credits, no papers, and no exams to write.

Rollins began by seeking out dynamic classroom teachers. He began locally with prize-winning DC-area professors but soon branched out, renting a studio and adding a video option to his early audio offerings. The company began to run searches nationwide for the people it now describes as "The Great Teachers." A TTC talent scout attended one of my lectures in 2000. She enjoyed it. So did the focus group to which she played a recording, and their approval led to an invitation to make a sample lecture. In those days the company was laboring in a pocket-handkerchief-sized studio in Springfield, Virginia, but it had already worked out an effective vetting and quality-control system.

I was delighted to survive the recruitment ordeal and to be contracted to make a series on American religious history, consisting of twenty-four half-hour lectures. Lecturing in the studio itself took a bit of getting used to. After teaching in classrooms where you monitor your students' expressions (puzzled, bored, animated) to see if they grasp your meaning, the big eye of a TV camera that offers no feedback feels rather cold. It's tough, also, to have before you a digital clock counting backwards from thirty minutes with the knowledge that your job is to end at the zero point, plus or minus a few seconds. Careful preparation and practice are essential. Because every series is marketed in both audio and video formats, you have to be sure that listeners don't feel they're missing anything. I learned not to say, "Look at this photograph of Billy Graham in 1951," but rather, "There is a photograph of Billy Graham, taken in 1951, which shows the young evangelist in full eloquent flow." Video customers get to see it; audio customers get to imagine it, and both are satisfied. All these matters can be learned and I, like most Teaching Company professors, soon got into the swing of lecturing to the big audience out there somewhere *beyond* the studio. I have now made six more courses for them and enjoy a steadily growing correspondence with interested customers. Homeschoolers swear by TTC courses, as do long-distance commuters. In fact the Teaching Company's thirty-minute lecture format is designed to fit the average American commute, as opposed to the fifty- or ninety-minute format used in most college classrooms.

As I began my first Teaching Company course, the producer reminded me, "Imagine that the audience is as highly educated as you are, but in other subjects." That was a useful piece of guidance; it gave me a feel for the kind of things I could expect them to grasp. Because TTC is a for-profit company, it does careful market research and knows a great deal about its audience; their ages, their professions, their incomes, and their other interests. A majority of them are already highly educated; most have postgraduate degrees and are fully acculturated to the idea of learning for its own sake. Before making any new course, TTC polls focus groups carefully to make certain there will be a profitable return on the investment. The company's extraordinary attention to quality and to careful research has enabled it to flourish and to outlast several competitors. Its studios today are ten times the size of those I visited a decade ago.

Lifelong learning is not just for landlubbers. It is also surging out into international waters on America's expanding fleet of cruise ships. There are cruises to suit every taste and pocketbook but most have found it worthwhile to have a few lecturers on every voyage, usually to offer highbrow morning fare before the evening shows, dances, and parties. I first lectured on Cunard's *Queen Elizabeth 2* in 2004 as it crossed the Atlantic Ocean from New York to Southampton. For a mixed audience of Americans and Brits my topic was the long history of Anglo-American relations, so calibrated as to offend the sensibilities of neither group when we got to the awkward events of 1776. With Cunard, with Silverseas, and with Royal Caribbean I've also lectured through the Panama Canal, on the Inside Passage up to the Alaska glaciers, and by the Azores in mid-Atlantic, always on geographically relevant topics. My shipboard audiences are very much the same kind of people who belong to the Buckhead Group and buy Teaching Company series: over fifty and nearly all drawn from the upper third of the whole population in terms of education and income. Perhaps the old Puritan spirit lives on in their belief that they must always be striving, even on vacation, and that a handful of entertaining lectures nicely answers to their consciences' demand for work as well as play.

Even people who never go to sea and don't actually buy adult education courses tend to pick up a little learning along the way. When my daughter went to Catholic school and word went around that I was a historian, I was sometimes asked to speak to groups that gathered immediately after one Mass and before the next on Sunday mornings. I remember researching a talk on "Good and Bad Popes of the Last Two Centuries" and having one audience member tell me, afterwards, "It had never really occurred to me that the popes all had long lives before they got the top job, and that there's plenty of scope for judging how well they managed along the way." That's the kind of delightful reaction I'm always looking for—the sudden jolt of recognition that things aren't preordained in the messy world of history (as opposed to the sanitized world of hagiography).

What are the future prospects for lifelong learning? I think they are immensely bright. Nearly half of all Americans get some liberal arts education in their late teens and early twenties but then go to work in jobs that use little or none of it. Their intellectual thirst has been stimulated but not satisfied, and many of them know it. The Internet, The Teaching Company, church groups, cruise programs, and distance-learning programs are giving ever-greater opportunities to ever-larger audiences. As more people live longer and healthier lives, in greater material security than ever before, they'll continue to seek out entertaining and informative teachers for the sheer pleasure of learning. Technology offers new avenues of access but that doesn't mean that individual teachers will ever go out of fashion. Students of all ages vote with their feet and still go "live" whenever possible. They know that there's no substitute for being in the actual physical presence of an enthusiastic flesh-and-blood teacher.

18: Death Be Not Chic

Judy Bachrach

"I've not given up thinking of death," said Levin. "It's true that it's high time I was dead; and that all this is nonsense. . . . I do value my ideas and my work awfully; but in reality only consider this: all this world of ours is nothing but a speck of mildew, which has grown up on a tiny planet . . . it's all dust and ashes."

I'VE BEEN LOOKING everywhere for a passage from a recent book, a scene from a film, or a television episode that approximates Tolstoy's take on death in *Anna Karenina*—that is, an up-to-date, accessible version not simply of what death (or dying) encompasses, but what it signifies in the larger scheme of things.

As Tolstoy noted in the passage above: death defines us. It's a serious business if only because it's the last business we shall ever perform, and how we perform it might well be beyond our control. If it is within our control, even if we manage to carry it off with what the nondead call "dignity" or "courage," how does that avail us? Whom does it benefit? Not the dead, certainly.

Death marks us permanently—and not simply because we are all, in another sense, marked men. Death defines who we are now and, inevitably, how we and our accomplishments will be considered at some later date most of us would generally prefer not to think about. At all.

However, this is not necessarily the approach popular culture chooses to take on the subject. Our culture doesn't ignore death. In modern films and on television dramas, it's everywhere: on fictive battlefields and in outer space; in the ER and the forensics lab; in the dire diagnoses of some crusty, limping doctor on a Fox network drama and ballooning from the plumped-up lips of brilliant babe doctors on *Grey's Anatomy*.

But here is the insurmountable problem: their kind of death is not death. Or to put it another way: the death you see on the screen will not be the death you have.

Let's start with movies, where death is presented in a manner as skewed (but slightly different) from the final act you see on TV. In films these days death is nothing special. Or rather, nothing *really* special. It is simply another in a series of exciting and quite attractive human events that will eventually yield—much like falling in love, weddings, births, or even a fight with your fiancé—a tempestuous but ultimately wonderfully satisfactory ending. Thus we have in the recent movie, *The Lovely Bones* (based on Alice Sebold's best-selling book of the same title) a story about a teenage murder victim who, despite the seeming finality of her fate, manages to watch over her family—and exact revenge on her killer—from some undisclosed location in the Great Beyond.

This isn't exactly a glossy new reflection on the nature of death. *The Lovely Bones* is only the most recent descendant of *Defending Your Life*, a comedy from 1991 starring Meryl Streep and Albert Brooks, described by Geffen Pictures as follows: "In an Afterlife resembling the present-day US, people must prove their worth by showing in court how they have demonstrated courage . . ." How is that for a comforting and culturally apt denouement? Americans will all, one day, find ourselves in the alternate universe of a heavenly courtroom! But *Defending Your Life* itself was a distant cousin of *Always*, a 1989 film starring Richard Dreyfuss as a lively but unfortunately dead pilot whose mortality seems to be in serious dispute. As the movie's tagline teased: "They couldn't hear him. They couldn't see him. But he was there when they needed him. Even after he was gone."

Even tepid conventional movies such as these have issues with the idea that death is . . . well . . . death. And finite. The 1998 film *Meet Joe Black*, whose entire plot was focused on the process of permanently expiring (a rarity for boffo prospects) had as its star a rather baby-faced Grim Reaper: Brad Pitt. Yes, in this movie Brad Pitt is Death, a circumstance that—if it turns out to be true—might certainly reshuffle a lot of our prejudices.

And why not? Death in this movie is in its own way just a comforting update of Tennessee Williams' Gentleman Caller: a young man who falls in love with the daughter of an incredibly rich tycoon (played in the film by Anthony Hopkins). And while by film's end we don't exactly get a voice-over narrative fit for the *New York Times'* "Vows" section ("Imagine my surprise when I found out what he really did for a living!"), the same sense of forced bemusement suffuses the whole picture.

Death, in other words, isn't some old coot with a scythe and a bad wardrobe: he's great in bed! He buys his clothes from Tom Ford! He's got a conscience! You can, without a moment's pang, invite him home to meet your parents—especially if there's a fair chance of a sizable inheritance from Dad.

Two years later, along came *Autumn in New York*, an updated version of *Love Story* (or perhaps *Terms of Endearment*) in which pretty Winona Ryder, age twenty-two and size 0, falls in love with a callous gray-haired playboy, played by Richard Gere. The startling plot twist? She's at death's door with a rare heart condition (there is never a lethal disease in a Hollywood screenplay that is merely garden-variety or dull), and he, despite being on the wrong side of fifty, is—oh, irony!—really hale. It was hardly an evolution from *Autumn* to *Dying Young*, a 1991 movie in which a character played by Julia Roberts nurses a fairly dim-witted stud (Campbell Scott) who does just that.

Recently, there has been one attempt by a filmmaker to grapple somewhat realistically with an insidious and fatal illness: the 2006 film *Away from Her*. The movie, based on a superb short story by Alice Munro, revolves around the effects of Alzheimer's disease. Three years ago, critics considered it a radical departure, a brilliant standout from the usual claptrap that involves fading away on screen. But was it really?

Alzheimer's is a devastating neurological disease I happen to know a good deal about, unfortunately. My mother has it. The first thing you lose is your memory and, along with it, any shred of common sense. You send cash via Western Union to complete strangers because these strangers promise to increase the sum a thousandfold. You confide in callers inquiring about your Social Security benefits and give out your bank details as well as your home address. You lose valuable items such as jewelry and accuse others of theft. Sometimes those others are in fact thieves. You never can tell. You never will really know. No one will.

Then you lose the rest of you, bit by bit: comprehension; special perception; relationships; personality—by which I mean your former personality. The old personality is replaced by a new quite unseemly and often terrifying personality, one that no one close to you recognizes. This new you may exhibit signs of paranoia, fear, violence, and finally the inability to do much of anything, including swallow.

Aside from the loss of memory, *Away from Her* included almost none of these symptoms. It starred the heartbreakingly beautiful Julie Christie, whose pale blue eyes and lofty cheekbones one can never stop watching, and whose acting skills have only heightened with maturity. She won a Golden Globe for Best Performance that year, and she more than deserved it.

But fair's fair. The movie, however exquisitely crafted and well interpreted, didn't really focus on the Alzheimer's victim Christie portrayed. It concentrated mainly on how Alzheimer's affected her husband (played by Gordon Pinsent). By mid-film, Christie was relegated to the back rooms of despair and disintegration—away from us, you might say.

The story then focused on the husband left behind. His misery. His betrayals. His need for love and consolation. And finally, the decisions he makes in the wake of losing his wife, even while she is living. In other words, he was spared. We were spared. The disease was permitted to take its toll, but it wreaked its devastation off-screen.

This is where the "honesty" of filmmaking deliberately denies reality. What I have learned about dying, after many years of hospice volunteer work and more than two years writing an advice column for the terminally ill and their relatives, is this: you don't look like Wynona Ryder while you're doing it. You won't be as hunky as Campbell Scott. You won't look like Debra Winger—no, not even Winger herself will look like Winger. The Winger we see on screen, her lips and cheeks dusted with floury powder to give her what Hollywood believes to be the verisimilitude of metastasized breast cancer, is not a reflection seen in any hospice mirror.

If your vital signs are failing, it is unlikely that you'll find a double of Jeremy Northam, from the CBS television show *Miami Medical*, whose character evidently never loses a patient, at your bedside. Dr. Gregory House will not be hanging around your hospital room saying, as he often does on the Fox show *House*: "Pretty much all the drugs I prescribe are addictive and dangerous." That's because, even when you don't have a hope of recovering, a fair number of real doctors are a lot more scared that you'll somehow get addicted in your last three days of life than concerned that you'll die in pain.

If you are taken to a trauma center, it will not be an environment like the one that you find on the NBC show *Trauma*, which is broadcast in defiance of the terrible ratings it receives, and where people like Dr. Nancy (played by Anastasia Griffith) recover quickly after being broadsided by an oncoming bus. Dr. Nancy had a ruptured spleen. In fact you may not recover at all. A ruptured spleen can lead to severe blood loss and death.

Here's what's probably going to happen if you have a long-term illness that, despite all efforts, spreads. Because of the pain medications administered, you will likely be very constipated and perhaps nauseous. The sicker you get, the less capable you will be of eating. You may have tubes in your throat that will prevent you from talking, so the probability of your delivering a series of invigorating and profound deathbed remarks to loving relatives, as seen, say, on NBC's show, *ER*, is minimal. Owing to the effects of medications, you might not even be conscious.

And those relatives gathered around your deathbed? They may not be so loving, when push comes to . . . um . . . shove. Even if they are loving, they might nonetheless want you to move on, as they like to say in our culture. So that they can.

In some sense our culture's fierce resistance to the bleak inevitable is understandable. Who is eager to experience the fear and impatience of bored relatives huddled together in the face of what one day they, too, will confront? Instead we get television episodes that mask finality, even while pretending to confront it, and films that gloss the ends of our lives with gold dust and perfume, giving us a finale as flimsy, fantastical, absurd, and gorgeous as their dewy-eyed stars. We watch these fictions so we *won't* have to think too much about death and, like Tolstoy's Levin, we tell ourselves, "So one goes on living, amusing oneself with hunting, with work—anything so as not to think of death!"

19: The American Dream, Twenty-Two Minutes at a Time

Paul Corrigan and Brad Walsh

THERE IS AN impolite term used in situation comedy writers' rooms called "schmuck-bait." (In truth, most of the terms used in sitcom writers' rooms are impolite.) Schmuck-bait is used to describe a series or character-altering plot twist that poses no real jeopardy. Will Sam Malone sell Cheers and use the money to open up a hat store? Will Raymond move a more comfortable distance from his mother? Of course not—only a schmuck would fall for an act break like that. Why? Because we all know that situation comedies always return to the status quo or the . . . well, situation.

Comedies are rarely serialized. Yes, there is some forward movement—Cousin Oliver moved in with the Bradys, and Niles married Daphne. But these changes usually occur well into a series when the writers are nearly out of stories. (Premise-altering plot twists look a lot more appealing when it's 12:30 in the morning, you haven't finished the draft for tomorrow's table read and you've pitched every idea you can think of only to hear the show-runner say, "Nope, they already did that on *South Park*.")

When a show is working, little if anything changes in the status quo. Despite this, week after week, the characters continue to try to escape their bonds. And, more interestingly, we the viewers continue to indulge these attempts. Why? Maybe it's because sitcoms reflect something unique about Americans and American culture. We are an aspirational people—just like our favorite sit-com characters. In life, we're aware that repeated failure can be a deterrent; it can undermine our sense of purpose. It can defeat even the most entrepreneurial among us. But in comedy it doesn't have to be that way. Failure is something to laugh off, to forget. Tomorrow will be another day.

An early example of this is one of the first real situation come-dies, *The Honeymooners*. The Kramdens and their upstairs neigh-bors, the Nortons, were constantly trying to improve their lot in life. The show was produced in the 1950s, but the Kramdens' apartment has none of the gadgets made popular in that decade. They have no refrigerator, no television, and they share a tele-phone with their neighbors, yet Ralph Kramden was forever striv-ing. He lived in a world where success wasn't just possible—it was only one invention, clever negotiating ploy with the boss, or good game of golf away. Like all good sitcom characters, Ralph always found himself back at square one, usually as a result of some fatal flaw in his personality, like stage fright or a bad temper.

In the episode "Opportunity Knocks But," Ralph hopes to turn a game of pool with the president of the bus company into a pro-motion. Instead, Ralph's best friend, Ed Norton, impresses Ralph's boss and Ed is offered the job of Ralph's dreams. Ralph is ready to throw in the towel. Ralph: "What's the use of kidding, Alice? You picked a loser. I'm never going to be any executive. I'm never going to be anything but a bus driver. Sixteen years I worked for that company. Where am I? Same spot I was in when I started. . . . I just haven't got it, that's all."

But a couple minutes later, in the same scene, Ralph is again full of hope, strutting around his sparsely decorated apartment, convinced that if he goes into the office tomorrow and explains to his boss that all of Ed's great ideas were actually his, he'll get the job instead of Ed. Spoiler alert—it doesn't work out that way.

This brings us to Ralph's other aspiration—to be a better man. *The Honeymooners* often ended with Ralph, hat in hand, apologizing to his wife for his shortcomings and promising to do better next time. Among these shortcomings was a slight tendency to threaten to punch his wife so hard she would enter a low earth orbit.

The other standout show of the 1950s is *I Love Lucy*. In many ways this show was the pioneer. It was the first show to shoot with three cameras, the first to shoot its scenes in sequence before an audience, the first to shoot on film, and the first to shoot in California. Lucy Ricardo wasn't happy just sitting at home. She wanted more. She wanted to be part of her husband's act. No matter how many times she found herself embarrassed or kicked out of the Tropicana, she believed if she worked hard enough, found just the right moment and the perfect hat, it would make the difference.

For aspirational comedies, though, there may be no better example than *The Beverly Hillbillies*, probably the most popular sitcom of the 1960s. The Clampett family struck oil in their backyard in the Ozarks and moved to Beverly Hills where they were welcomed because of their wealth. What they aspired to is a certain kind of social acceptance and California was the place for it. There was no aristocracy guarding the gates; in fact, the people of Beverly Hills tripped over themselves to try to get a piece of the Clampetts' oil money. In the series pilot, before meeting the Clampetts, Mr. Drysdale, the banker, says, "I know to the dollar what kind of people they are. They're my kind of people—loaded."

New money is just as good as old money in America. Social mobility is as easy as packing up the car and moving. The only thing keeping a family from joining high society is an oil strike. And an oil strike can easily be replaced with a new business or invention. In fact, all you have to do is change oil to Prohibition era whiskey, and the family might even produce a president.

Moving into the 1970s, more workplace comedies began to appear, particularly ones with single people trying to make it on their own. *Mary Tyler Moore*, as groundbreaking as it may have been, was still a show with an aspirational character at its core.

Mary Richards moved out on her own to work hard and build a career. A *woman* living on her own and having a career may have been out of the norm at the time, but it was something everyone could identify with because her goals of independence and success were shared by everyone in the audience.

Redd Foxx's character on *Sanford and Son* was a throwback to Ralph Kramden, with just as many money-making schemes that went nowhere. Instead of living in a modest apartment full of junk, Sanford lived in an actual junkyard. There was no place for him to go but up, and he kept hoping he would. On *Taxi*, most of the characters believed driving a taxi was a stepping-stone. It was just a way to pay the bills until they moved on to bigger and better things.

And if you were looking for aspiration, who could top Alex P. Keaton from the 1980s' hit *Family Ties*?

Today, *The Office*'s Michael Scott is a man who believes that success is only an inspirational poster away. He is always going to try to be a better boss and move up the corporate ladder but will always wind up back where he started.

Why do sitcoms seem to so well represent this aspirational aspect of American culture? Looking at how sitcoms are produced can help shed some light on this. Most sitcoms get their start in late summer. Thousands of writers head to studio offices to pitch their idea for the next hit. Usually they walk out of the office with no real indication of whether the studio wants to buy it or not. All they have to show for their efforts is a complimentary bottle of Fiji water, and all they can do is wait.

The writers who get past this stage move on to pitching their idea to a network. This leads to another round of waiting. Getting past this hurdle means beginning work on an outline and then on a script—getting notes at every stage. Usually just after New Year's the script is due (a schedule seemingly designed to ensure no writer ever enjoys Christmas). Then more waiting begins.

At this point the lucky ones are told they won't be producing a pilot. The even luckier ones get acceptance letters to law school and never have to go through the process again. For the last few months they have been on countless phone calls telling them what is wrong with what they are doing and how the studio or network wants it modified. These conversations are peppered with words and phrases like "proactive," "likeable," "larger than life," "work-family balance."

Where these terms come from no one knows. And if most people are being honest, they have very little idea what they mean, or at least how they help you write jokes about a wacky neighbor. Most people put up with these conversations because they help sell a show.

The Hollywood writers who get the green light to produce a show are faced with more meetings, more conference calls, casting, and the list goes on. Writers put up with all this because of one man—Desi Arnaz. Back in the 1950s Arnaz made one of the best deals in television history. In return for covering the extra production cost of shooting *I Love Lucy* on film, he was given ownership of the film. The reruns of *I Love Lucy* produced a flood of money. And every sitcom writer since then has dreamed of creating a show that lasts long enough to reach syndication and produce a similar flood.

Despite the free lunches and the ability to go to work in sneakers and a T-shirt, sitcom writers are just like most Americans and just like the characters they write. They aspire to better things. Most will never achieve the success they dream of, but they spend year after year going through the same process and believing that their windfall is just one great pitch away. Sure they make fun of schmuck-bait. But they fall for it every time.

Sitcoms, whether we're writing them or watching them, bring Americans a certain degree of comfort. While our worlds are in constant motion—particularly thanks to modern technology—and we often feel as though the rug could be pulled from under us at any moment, sitcoms promise stability. The characters will largely behave the same from week to week. The sets will not change much and neither will the setups. That they're on at the same time every week is even a way to mark time. They're a reason to gather with family and friends on a set schedule.

But the fact that the characters are always trying to break out of that world—that Ralph Kramden is always trying to be a better husband, that Michael Scott is always trying to be a better boss—to bring about some fundamental change is touching. One man's aspiration is another one's inspiration.

20: Utopian Virtues

Caitrin Nicol

IN THE DECADES just prior to the Civil War, with a large blot spreading on the national conscience and industrialization beginning to show its mechanical face, utopian communes popped up like mushrooms on the American landscape. Shutting out society's corruption, soullessness, and original sin, Transcendentalists and other visionaries sought purity by reconnecting with the land, as if they could reclaim a state of innocence merely by scratching at the soil.

This impulse to escape and start anew has reappeared throughout American history, from Brook Farm and Fruitlands to New Harmony and Walden Pond. Today, popular culture frequently draws upon this impulse to explore the modern condition, either to criticize it for its excesses or to highlight its peculiar fears and anxieties. In the process, storytellers and filmmakers raise provocative questions about the development of virtues such as perseverance in the face of suffering and death, and challenge us to consider how the technological triumphs of modernity relate to the formation of character.

Such an experiment in pastoral nostalgia is the subject of a haunting movie, *The Village*, directed by M. Night Shyamalan. Shyamalan is known for making supernatural thrillers with a metaphysical twist, as he did in *The Sixth Sense*, but in *The Village* he subsumes the supernatural for drama on a human scale.

The film tells the love story of Ivy Walker, a blind tomboy, and Lucius Hunt, a contemplative young man, who live in a dreamy nineteenth-century hamlet. Their village is cut off from the outside world by Covington Woods, which, the film suggests, contains one kind of menace and separates them from another. Out beyond the woods are "the towns," reported to be "wicked places where wicked people live," but no one born in the village has ever left it and seen them.

A more immediate threat lurks just inside the forest—creatures too dreadful to be named that are kept at bay by elaborate security precautions. Yellow flags and watchtowers along the perimeter ratify a provisional truce: we do not disturb them and they will not disturb us. The color red belongs to "Those We Do Not Speak Of" and must not be found in any form within the precincts of the village or "they" will be attracted to it. Warning bells, safety drills, and ritual peace offerings serve to remind the villagers of their constant peril.

This pervasive menace seems hatched from a fairy tale—and, in fact, that is what it is. The children of the village, who have never known another life, could not be expected to appreciate the vileness of something as abstract as the towns, and so the elders devise a myth complete with daily rituals to guard the innocence of their children. This mythology also allows the elders to avoid mentioning those they *really* do not speak of—the siblings, spouses, and parents they lost to violent crime before fleeing society and coming to rebuild on their own. "There is no one in this village who has not lost someone irreplaceable, who has not felt loss so deeply that they questioned the very merit of living at all," Ivy's father, Edward, the chief elder, confesses to her in a moment of anguish. "It is a darkness I wished you would never know."

This wish has been a mirage. "You may run from sorrow, as we have," another elder mutters to an uncomprehending Lucius. "Sorrow will find you. It can smell you." He has just buried his seven-year-old son. The event is all more poignant because in the outside world it is actually the twenty-first century, and there the child could almost certainly have been saved.

As the movie progresses we learn that the village elders met each other at a Philadelphia grief counseling center in the 1970s, each of them shattered by the murder of a loved one. Unwilling to continue living in a world they felt was irredeemably broken by violence, they retreated to a time in which they believed such violence could not happen. While trying to get on the other side of original sin is a doomed endeavor, they do succeed in escaping many of the vices of modernity: the closeness of their community, their lack of cynicism, their simplicity and humble gratitude, and their spontaneous joy—these are the features of their new society, a marked contrast to the old one. They have apparently been reconciled to the hard bargain they set for themselves with the idea that death and disease, and the sorrow that accompanies them, are *natural*, and there is an essential purity in this.

It is this idealized vision of innocence that serves as their touchstone. "That, in the end, is what we have protected here: *innocence*," insists one elder. "What was the purpose of our leaving? Let us not forget—it was out of *hope* of something *good* and *right*." That hope, which comes at the cost of lying to their children, is that their protected world is one without evil.

Evil creeps back in the way it always comes: not by social forces but by individual desires. Eventually, the community experiences a violent crime that leaves Lucius seriously wounded. Ivy's father breaks the compact and endangers their way of life by allowing her to set out through the woods to retrieve medicine. Defending his decision to the other elders, he protests, "The world moves for love. It kneels before it in awe." This too is a myth—one of such staggering loveliness that it might be worth every other lie of the experiment. If it were true, of course, they would have no reason to be there—their murdered relatives were beloved, too, and the "world" didn't give a damn. But if the world doesn't, *they* do—they *choose to live* that way, and for that reason it is true in the confines of their creation. In their world, they kneel for love, and thus it seems as if the world is kneeling.

Ultimately, that world is perpetuated by a grimmer lie: Ivy succeeds in fetching medicine for Lucius but along the way kills someone in self-defense, mistaking him for one of Those We Do Not Speak Of. The elders determine to use this misinterpretation to cement the myth in the minds of the younger villagers forever. As troubling as it is, their decision to do this is also strangely moving. A deep desire for purity, such as they have, is the mainspring of any number of virtues and the haunting beauty of their world. But their overallegiance to what is in and of itself a good thing comes at an appalling cost.

There was some chatter when the film was released about whether Shyamalan had stolen his conceit from Margaret Peterson Haddix's 1995 young-adult novel *Running Out of Time*. The essential similarity is that there is a nineteenth-century village located, unbeknownst to most of its residents, in the present day, and when there is a medical emergency a teenage girl sets off for the outside world in search of help. Beyond that, the stories lead in different directions. Rather than the desperate idea of a group of broken people, Haddix's Clifton Village is a kind of theme park—a historical attraction where visitors can view live footage, via *Truman Show*–like hidden cameras, of a "real" 1840 community.

The adults' motivation for participating was varied—they included neo-Puritans, radical environmentalists, people seeking a clean break with the confusion of their current lives, and people simply attracted to the romance of the past—but all were so deeply dissatisfied with modernity that it seemed sufficient reason to raise their children in a quaint, exploitative environment. The deal was supposed to be that they would still have access to modern medical care, but when their corporate backers choke it off, a diphtheria epidemic breaks out. Jessie Keyser, thirteen, makes a daring escape to fetch help, running out of her own time as time is running out.

There is a kind of cognitive dissonance about this story, insofar as the backdrop to Jessie's adventure—the people left behind in Clifton responding to the crisis as best they can—would actually make for an inspiring narrative had it *really* been set a century or two ago. The extremity of the situation seems to draw out the best or worst in everyone. On the honorable side there is a great deal of valor, grit, self-sacrifice, and—when there is nothing else left—hope. There is a wonderful moment toward the end where Jessie and her sister Hannah, reunited, trade stories of trying to fill each other's shoes: Jessie remembering to be prudent like Hannah would be, Hannah finding the courage to do something she didn't think that she was brave enough to do herself by pretending to be Jessie.

But the irony is that the whole ordeal was totally unnecessary. There is a great lesson in the way that virtue can transcend adversity, but adversity is not chosen, not to mention manufactured, for the sake of the virtue it might summon. Jessie's and Hannah's heroism is no less genuine for the artificial adversity—they are not responsible for their strange circumstances, after all—but there is a cloud over it. With the discovery of vaccines and penicillin, diphtheria became avoidable, and so a failure to avoid it now means something different than it did in 1840. Potential triumphs of *psyche* were irreversibly displaced by a triumph of *techne*.

The point to consider is how far that displacement carries, or should carry, into situations that are less morally straightforward. What if all of our physical challenges, which people once understood as tests of character, could be technologically resolved? Is it conscionable to accept peril when we have the power not to?

That premise (or its negation) lies at the center of many futurist utopias, and in Lois Lowry's book, *The Giver*, which won the Newbery Medal in 1994, it is manifested as a perfectly and pleasantly flat society. There is no aspiration because there is nothing

to aspire to; all struggles have been scientifically or socially leveled. Everyone leads a safe, cheerful, comfortable life. There is
nothing to cast a shadow and nowhere to cast it.

"I tried to seduce the reader," Lowry explained in her Newbery
acceptance speech, and "I seduced myself along the way. It did
feel good, that world. I got rid of all the things I fear and dislike;
all the violence, prejudice, poverty, and injustice, and I even threw
in good manners as a way of life because I liked the idea of it. One
child has pointed out, in a letter, that the people in [that] world
didn't even have to do dishes. It was very, very tempting to leave
it at that."

In this society, there is a place called "Elsewhere," an all-pur-
pose repository for anything different or unknown. Even history
belongs to Elsewhere. It falls to one select person, the "Receiver
of Memories," to hold in trust all the painful, foreign, exhilarating recollections of the old world—ours—from once upon a very
remote time. As the book begins, the twelve-year-old Jonas is chosen to become the new Receiver, to absorb memories one by one
from his predecessor. These memories reveal to him how (and
why) his world was leveled, and how all its familiar features are no
more than skeletal representations of what used to be.

His little sister Lily has a "comfort object" that he comes to recognize as an *elephant*. He has never seen an animal in real life,
but in the memories, he witnesses a group of men fell one of these
great creatures on the savanna and make off with its tusks in a
Jeep, while another one emerges from the brush to stroke its com-
panion, bellowing in grief and rage. Jonas tries to share this revelation with his sister: "Not of the tortured cry of the elephant, but
of the *being* of the elephant, of the towering, immense creature
and the meticulous touch with which it had tended its friend at
the end." But to Lily and to everyone else, this sensational tableau
has been collapsed into an inanimate stuffed lump.

If the memories show Jonas the depth floating underneath his
two-dimensional life, they also lead him to discover pockets of

gloom tucked into the utopia itself. The anguish voiced by the surviving elephant—where is it now? Gone, of course. No one would choose to include such experiences in an ideal world. And in order to eliminate bereavement, the utopian designers naturally had to attack its source.

In Jonas's community, references to death are euphemistic to the point of total abstraction. On the very rare occasion that there is an accident, it is called a "Loss." The community gathers to chant the lost person's name, fading away to silence; the name is then recycled and given to a new baby. For everyone else, there is "release." The ill, the old, the defective, the troublesome are all quietly released to Elsewhere, as Jonas is aghast to learn, by means of lethal injection. (*The Giver* was Lowry's second Newbery winner. Her first, *Number the Stars*, is the story of a girl in Copenhagen in 1943, whose friends and neighbors begin to be mysteriously "relocated." This historical example was surely on the author's mind as she wrote about release. Scrubbing out the "wrong" kind of people, including the infirm, is an all-too-familiar approach to advancing an idealized social vision. There is not much distance between the impulse to *fix* and to *remove*.)

The designers have succeeded in expunging death entirely from lived experience. But to gain control of it, they have to actively administer it, in *their* way, on *their* terms, in *their* time. They kill in order to avoid mentioning or thinking about death at all.

Curiously, the approach to controlling emotions, those former rascally agents of chaos, is just the reverse: they are plastered out in the open in a mandatory daily "sharing of feelings." Stronger ones are dulled with medication, and the rest dissipate into thin air. *Eros*, like all other kinds of yearning, belongs to Elsewhere. "Love" is a rude word, uncomfortable. But Jonas loves—and when he finds out that his beloved baby foster brother is scheduled for release, he takes him and flees.

Thus Jonas makes a reverse escape, running from the painless future, just as Ivy and Jessie ran from the innocent past, all with a courage born of love, and all in search of somewhere very like the present—the very place that their ancestors decided, on behalf of all of their descendants, to abandon for a man-made paradise.

As a kind of blessing before every meal, Shyamalan's villagers say, "We are grateful for the time we have been given." In a way, this is disingenuous, as the time that they were really given was the one that they rejected; but the deeper lesson is their humble recognition that all time is borrowed. Seeking to escape chaos and suffering by idealizing the past or the future is, in the end, a rejection of our responsibility to the short bit of time that is ours, and a denial of our natures that aspire toward virtue even as they incline toward sin.

21: Never Having to Say You're Sorry
The Challenges of Forgiveness in an Age of Relativism

Chuck Colson

Forgive us our trespasses, as we forgive those who trespass
against us. —Matthew 6:12

THERE ARE MOMENTS in history when the goodness of
humanity brilliantly illuminates the darkness. June 1, 2010,
was just such a moment. The place, appropriately, was one of the
darkest cities in America—Detroit, ravaged by the collapse of the
automobile industry.

At Comerica Park, the Detroit Tigers' Armando Galarraga was
pitching. The crowd fell silent as Galarraga—a young man who
had been slated to be sent to the minor leagues—retired the first
twenty-six batters. He was on the verge of making baseball history. Only twenty perfect games have ever been pitched.

Galarraga was one out away from throwing the twenty-first.
With two outs in the ninth, the Cleveland Indians batter hit an
easy grounder to the Tiger first baseman. Galarraga, the pitcher,
raced to cover first. It's a routine play; Galarraga and the ball
reached first base at least a step ahead of the runner. Galarraga
was about to become a baseball immortal.

Except he didn't. "Safe!" shouted umpire Jim Joyce. Galarraga's
response was a simple smile—a smile that, as Joe Posnanski of
Sports Illustrated said, seemed to ask, "Are you sure? I really hope
you are sure."

The blown call outraged fans across the country. For Joyce's part, as soon as he saw the replay, he knew that he had gotten it wrong. He told reporters, "I just cost that kid a perfect game."

By baseball standards, such an admission was extraordinary: umpires are paid to make judgment calls and stand by them. Players and managers can argue with them but only within limits, and with no expectation of having the call reversed.

So when Joyce apologized to Galarraga, we were already in unfamiliar territory. When Galarraga, in turn, forgave Joyce, adding that the umpire probably felt worse than he did and that "nobody's perfect," we were witnessing something extraordinary.

The victim of what Posnanski calls one of the "most absurd injustices in the history of baseball" went out of his way to comfort the umpire who made the mistake. And the umpire was humble enough to ask for forgiveness. It was a spontaneous, unforgettable moment.

The ability to forgive is one of the most powerful forces for good in any society. It can reconcile the most grievous altercations, which are an ever-present reality in a fallen world. Forgiveness brings about *shalom*—the biblical term for concord and harmony—between people who have the greatest differences imaginable and can transform institutions and even warring nations.

America is rightly known for its forgiving nature. The land of second chances, we like to say. What other nation in history has simultaneously fought major world wars against two mighty military powers—Japan and Germany—eventually conquered its attackers, and then turned right around to rebuild the very countries it fought?

And yet in recent years, Americans have become a deeply cynical and unforgiving people. A 1988 Gallup poll revealed that 50 percent of Americans do not believe that they could forgive others; another revealed that "forgiveness is something virtually all Americans aspire to" (94 percent) but "is not something we frequently offer." Only 48 percent acknowledged attempting to forgive others. And yet, as Melissa Healy, in the *Los Angeles Times'* article "The Science of Forgiveness" (January 6, 2008) noted a few years ago, a refusal to forgive those who have harmed us can increase the risk of heart attacks and depression.

How and why did we reach this tragic place?

Some saw this sad state of affairs coming. In 1973 psychiatrist Karl Menninger wrote a popular book titled *Whatever Happened to Sin?* Good question. What happened is that sin has become the most politically incorrect subject we can possibly raise in polite company, because it involves being judgmental.

But a society that doesn't take sin seriously has difficulty taking forgiveness seriously: after all, if nobody does anything wrong, there's nothing to forgive.

The consequences of this are compounded by the long-running series of public transgressions, from the granddaddy of all scandals—Watergate—to the savings and loan scandals, Enron, Wall Street, and a raft of "pro-family" lawmakers like Governor Mark Sanford being caught in adulterous affairs.

This parade of offenses, besides giving hypocrisy—the tribute vice pays to virtue—a bad name, has inured people, turning us into a nation of cynics. Americans have become accustomed to the stage-managed, scripted public apology. Americans have come to recognize that those doing the apologizing seem to be a lot sorrier for having been caught than for engaging in sinful behavior.

Consider the case of golfer Tiger Woods, who was forced to reveal that he had been unfaithful to his wife. I watched as Woods stood in front of the cameras and gave a tortured attempt at an apology. And then, in a monotone, with all the emotion of a marionette on a string, he asked for forgiveness. But his effort fell flat, because it was clear that he was reading from a script. No questions were allowed.

For me and millions of others, I suspect, it was shattering to watch. This young man was tutored by his dad, close to his own family—so it seemed—and a great role model. Why couldn't he face up to his failure and ask God and his family and his fans to forgive him? There was not a hint of authenticity. This may be why Woods continued to lose endorsements and why few people showed much sympathy toward him.

The difference between Tiger Woods and umpire Jim Joyce is sincerity. Joyce did not have to apologize, and yet he did—with deep regret for a mistake any umpire could have made. And because his apology was sincerely offered, Armando Galarraga accepted it, willingly forgiving someone who had done him harm.

But with such widespread public cynicism, many Americans no longer recognize genuine repentance when they see it, never mind offer sincere forgiveness. I've experienced this. Five years after Watergate I was invited to appear on the *Phil Donahue* show. By then I had been working in the prisons for about four years. My conversion to Christianity had been well publicized, and I had made public statements of genuine repentance.

But that day I ran into a buzz saw of hatred. When Donahue made a particularly condemning statement, the audience would erupt in catcalls. Donahue really baited me. When I tried to answer his questions, he cut me off. One working-class woman in the audience got up and said, "I don't understand all you big shots. You get into big trouble and you steal us poor people blind. And then you claim to have found religion, and now you've got God on your side. Why don't you guys just find God and go home and be quiet?"

The audience cheered wildly. I was upset because while I knew my conversion was sincere, I also knew there was no way I was going to convince this woman. And I understand why in the succeeding years the cynicism has only deepened.

But I wish that woman, and so many others, could come with me into America's prisons where she would witness what is missing in our culture. I've seen extraordinary examples of repentance, forgiveness, and reconciliation behind prison walls—dark, dank places that are Satan's playground.

For instance, many years ago, a young woman named Dee Dee Washington sat in a car waiting for her boyfriend, a young man who, unbeknownst to Dee Dee, was purchasing drugs. The boyfriend got into an altercation with the drug dealer, whose name was Ron Flowers. Racing from the scene, Ron pulled out a gun and shot Dee Dee as she waited in the car. She died of her wounds, and Flowers was convicted of her murder.

For fourteen years, Ron denied killing Dee Dee. But then he became involved in Prison Fellowship's ministry. In our Inner-Change Freedom Initiative (IFI), offenders are confronted with the harm they have done to their victims and families of victims.

Ron finally admitted to the murder. He then wrote to Dee Dee's mother, Anna Washington, expressing deep remorse for his crime. Every year of Ron's sentence, Mrs. Washington had written to the parole board urging them to deny him parole. However, the week Ron confessed, Mrs. Washington felt an overwhelming conviction that she should meet with the man who killed her daughter.

When the visit was arranged, a repentant Ron told Mrs. Washington how he had come to kill her precious daughter, and he asked to be forgiven. Mrs. Washington took his hands in hers. "I forgive you," she said.

I attended Ron's graduation service in the prison. As he was walking toward me to receive his certificate I saw out of the corner of my eye a tall, handsome, African American woman stand up in the crowd and come toward us. She threw her arms around Ron and announced, "I am the mother of the young girl that Ron murdered." She proceeded to tell the stunned crowd the story, and ended by declaring, "This young man is my adopted son."

After his release, Mrs. Washington helped Ron Flowers adjust to life back in the community, invited him over for dinner, and even attended his wedding. This beautiful ending to a tragic story could only happen through God's grace. Only he can bring about such reconciliation and healing.

The ability to recognize serious wrongs as such, and then to be able to turn the other cheek and forgive—that takes God's transforming power. I'm not talking about what Dietrich Bonhoeffer called cheap grace, in which one immediately and unthinkingly dispenses with a serious transgression. I'm talking about the kind of offenses people agonize over. I have witnessed forgiveness leading even warring nations to work toward real peace and reconciliation.

In Northern Ireland, "the Troubles" began in August of 1969 when British troops marched onto the streets of Belfast and Londonderry. Then came Bloody Sunday: January 30, 1972. British soldiers, attempting to break up a civil-rights rally in Londonderry, shot and killed fourteen demonstrators, some of them teenagers. The killings set off waves of retaliatory violence. Those who survived each new blast lived in fear of the next attack by Irish Republican Army terrorists. In just three years over a thousand Protestants and Catholics were killed.

When I first visited Belfast in 1977, nearly every block contained bomb-blackened, boarded up buildings. Police stations of the Royal Ulster Constabulary were fortresses rolled in barbed wire, their thick, high walls tented with steel mesh to guard against the terrorists' habit of lobbing homemade bombs over the walls. One exploded as I was standing less than a block away. Terror was an ever-present reality.

On a subsequent visit I went to the notorious Maze Prison and befriended inmates on both sides who refused to talk with one another. I listened to the stories, not only of the Catholic and Protestant inmates, but also of their victims and their families.

There was Liam McCloskey who, for much of his violent young life, had been a member of the Irish National Liberation Army (INLA), a Marxist offshoot of the IRA. Convicted of armed hijacking and robbery, Liam was serving a ten-year sentence at Maze. He took part in a hunger strike in 1981, going without food for fifty-five days. Lying in a hospital bed, Liam began to pray. *There has to be a God*, he thought. "Life makes no sense without one.

Can I go before God with nothing but a self-centered life of striving after sex, drink, and good times? And what about my involve-
ment in Republicanism?"

On Day 55 Liam's mother arrived and tearfully told him that
when he entered a coma, she would have him fed intravenously.
She pleaded with him to end the strike immediately so that his
starvation-induced blindness would not become permanent. He
reluctantly agreed. As he recovered, Liam continued to think
about God and the truths he had discovered on his hunger strike.
He realized he could not walk the way of Republicanism and the
way of Jesus at the same time; he had to choose.

"I took the way of Jesus," Liam told me. "I began to realize that
God loved me and I loved God." He resigned from the INLA and
determined to become a force for reconciliation.

His first effort was to join Protestant prisoners in the prison dining room, breaking the self-imposed segregation between Catholics and Protestants. There, Liam met Jimmy Gibson, a Protestant
paramilitary member serving time for attempted murder. Jimmy
couldn't wait to go after Catholic paramilitaries when he got out
of prison. Partly because of his inner turmoil, and partly through
Liam's influence, Jimmy instead gave his life to Jesus and joined a
Bible study with those who had once been his sworn enemies.

Like Liam, Jimmy began learning how to forgive and seek reconciliation rather than plot revenge. Each participant would confess
his sins against the other side and experience incredible healing.

One evening, as the Bible study met for prayer, they came upon
the name of a young girl at the top of the list: Karen McKeown,
a Protestant who was deeply committed to serving Christ. While
working at her church one evening, Karen had been shot by an
INLA terrorist. Liam, as a former member of the INLA, felt a
special responsibility for Karen's suffering and had written to her
mother.

A few days later, when Karen finally died after weeks of suffering, Liam wrote again to Karen's mother, Pearl McKeown.

"Pearl, we make strange friends in this troubled land," Liam wrote. "It is to the glory of God and He who makes it possible. Remember John 8:51, 'And I tell you most solemnly. Whoever keeps My Word will never see death.' Karen has left us, and even though it was no choice of mine, yet you can make a conscious decision in your own mind to see it as a gift of God. Your beautiful daughter to our beautiful Father who knows best. Surely the peace of Christ will be yours."

I returned to Belfast some years later in 1983 to attend Prison Fellowship's first international conference. The highlight came one evening during a meeting open to the public. Some eight hundred townspeople—both Protestant and Catholic—streamed into Queen's University's elegant Whitlow Hall, the space donated for the occasion. Clearly, our ministry in Northern Ireland's prisons had captured the interest of many of Ulster's citizens.

Liam McCloskey and Jimmy Gibson had been furloughed from prison to be with us for the week. Their presence, more than anything else, evidenced the reconciling power of the gospel. That evening, each told how he had come to know Christ. Liam concluded by putting his thin arm around Jimmy's muscular shoulders.

"My hope is to believe that God is changing the hearts of men like myself and Jimmy," Liam said. "That's the only hope I have for peace in Northern Ireland. Before, if I had seen Jimmy on the street, I would have shot him. Now he's my brother in Christ. I would die for him."

As members of the audience murmured in disbelief, James McIlroy, director of Prison Fellowship for Northern Ireland, took the microphone. "There's a woman I'd like you to meet," he said, motioning to someone in the back row.

A lithe, energetic woman, Pearl McKeown, began to thread her way toward the front. As she did, James briefly told the story of Pearl and Karen McKeown; of Karen's death at the hands of an

INLA gunman; of Pearl's friendship through the mail with Liam, the former INLA terrorist; and how Pearl and Liam had grown to love one another as mother and son, though they had never met.

Pearl climbed the stage steps and walked slowly toward Liam, arms outstretched. They hugged. Then Pearl held Liam's hand as she tearfully explained how Karen's death had been to God's glory.

"Liam told me his prayer is now that of St. Francis," she said. "'Lord, make me an instrument of your peace.' And Liam has been God's instrument of peace to me," she concluded in a choked voice. "For he is the one who has showed me how to love God again."

By now tears glistened in many eyes as the audience strained to capture the incredible tableau: the two former paramilitary members, one Catholic, one Protestant, once sworn enemies, now standing together as brothers in Christ; the bereaved Protestant mother and the former Catholic terrorist, holding hands. I saw eight undred people in tears, standing and cheering at first, but then simply watching with deep emotion as this healing took place. It was a moment of hope, a joyful wedge thrust into forty years of religious hate and bitterness. I'd never seen anything like it.

Afterward, a small army of Christian volunteers, both Catholic and Protestant, began organizing into groups. They worked in all of the prisons in Northern Ireland and marched for peace. On one visit I had to be searched by the British troops before I could enter the Catholic part of Londonderry. But there I found a hall full of Catholics and Protestants singing praise songs together— something that a few years ago would have been unthinkable.

The movement that began in the prisons began to spread to churches. Groups of Protestants and Catholics began to meet, march together, and conduct rallies for peace.

Ultimately, the private acts of forgiveness, which blossomed into a full-blown movement, led to public consequences. On April 10, 1998—Good Friday—Britain and Northern Ireland reached a peace and power-sharing agreement. British troops began to withdraw and peace broke out in Northern Ireland—shaky at first, but peace nonetheless.

I recalled that electrifying moment in a Belfast prison in June of 2010, when newly elected British prime minister David Cameron publically apologized to the people of Northern Ireland for the 1972 Bloody Sunday killings, calling them "both unjustified and unjustifiable."

"What happened should never, ever have happened," Cameron said. "The families of those who died should not have had to live with the pain and hurt of that day and a lifetime of loss. Some members of our armed forces acted wrongly. The government is ultimately responsible for the conduct of the armed forces. And for that, on behalf of the government—and indeed our country—I am deeply sorry."

I watched Cameron's apology on television. Tears came to my eyes as I watched Belfast factory workers stopping to listen, and then weeping or jumping for joy. I watched as Londoners stood in the rain, listening with tears on their cheeks. Clearly, they all knew genuine repentance when they saw it.

No one witnessing that scene could deny that the greatest power on earth is love. It is demonstrated most dramatically when we learn how to love our enemies—when we learn to repent, accept forgiveness, and learn how to forgive others.

Contributors

DANIEL AKST is a member of the editorial board at *Newsday* whose work has appeared in the *New York Times, Wall Street Journal, Los Angeles Times, Boston Globe, Slate,* and other leading publications. His latest book is *We Have Met the Enemy: Self-Control in an Age of Excess.*

PATRICK ALLITT is a professor at Emory University and the author of five books on aspects of American political and religious history, most recently, *The Conservatives: Ideas and Personalities Throughout American History.* He is also author of a book about his life as a professor: *I'm the Teacher, You're the Student: A Semester in the University Classroom.*

JUDY BACHRACH, a contributing editor at *Vanity Fair,* is a longtime hospice volunteer who has been answering questions from readers about death or dying for the past three years on her website (www.thecheckoutline.org) as well as on www.obit-mag.com.

MEGAN BASHAM is the senior entertainment reporter and critic for *World Magazine* and the author of *Beside Every Successful Man,* a work that examines how wives impact their husband's professional achievements. She has also written for outlets like the *Wall Street Journal,* the *Weekly Standard,* and *National Review.* Megan has appeared as a guest on *Today,* Fox News, and MSNBC.

MARK BAUERLEIN is a professor of English at Emory University, and has recently served as director of the Office of Research and Analysis at the National Endowment for the Arts. His books include *The Dumbest Generation: How the Digital Age Stupefies Young Americans and Jeopardizes Our Future* and *Literary Criticism: An Autopsy.*

PIA CATTON is an arts reporter and columnist for the *Wall Street Journal*'s Greater New York section. She has served as the features editor at Politico and the cultural editor at the *New York Sun.*

CHUCK COLSON is a popular and widely known author, speaker, and radio commentator. A former presidential aide to Richard Nixon and founder of Prison Fellowship, BreakPoint, and the Chuck Colson Center for Christian Worldview, he has written many books, including *Born Again, Loving God, How Now Shall We Live?, The Good Life*, and *The Faith Given Once, for All.* His weekday radio broadcast, *BreakPoint*, airs to 2 million listeners.

PAUL CORRIGAN is a television writer and producer. He has written for shows on Fox, ABC, NBC, and CBS. His credits include *Married... with Children* and *King of the Hill*, for which he received an Emmy nomination. He is currently a co-executive producer of ABC's *Modern Family*, for which he has won the Writers Guild award for Outstanding New Series as well as an Emmy award for Outstanding Comedy Series.

CAITLIN FLANAGAN is an award-winning journalist who has been a contributing editor for the *Atlantic* and a staff writer for the *New Yorker*. Her books include *To Hell with All That: Loving and Loathing Our Inner Housewife* and the forthcoming *Girl Land*, which is an exploration of the emotional lives of pubescent girls.

MEGHAN COX GURDON is an essayist, book critic, and former foreign correspondent whose work appears regularly in the *Wall Street Journal*, where she writes a bimonthly column about children's literature. She also writes a light, twice-weekly column about social and domestic affairs for the *Washington Examiner*.

MARGO HOWARD writes the advice column *Dear Margo*, which is syndicated in two hundred newspapers, and on-line at www .wowowow.com. Her most recent book is *A Life in Letters: Ann Landers' Letters to Her Only Child*.

KAY S. HYMOWITZ is the William E. Simon Fellow at the Manhattan Institute and a contributing editor of *City Journal*. Hymowitz is the author, most recently, of *Marriage and Caste in America: Separate and Unequal Families in a Post-Marital Age*.

JONATHAN V. LAST is a senior writer at the *Weekly Standard*. From 2006 through 2008, he was a columnist for the *Philadelphia Inquirer*. His writings have appeared in the *Wall Street Journal*, the *Los Angeles Times*, the *Washington Post*, the *Claremont Review of Books*, *First Things*, and elsewhere.

HERB LONDON is president of the Hudson Institute. He is professor emeritus at New York University where he was founder and dean of the Gallatin School. London is the author and editor of twenty-four books including his most recent ones, *Diary of a Dean* and *Decline and Revival in Higher Education*.

STACY LONDON is one of America's premier style experts, best known from TLC's *What Not to Wear*. She has appeared on various national TV shows including *Today*, *Oprah*, *Access Hollywood*, Fox News, CNN, and many more. She is the author of *Dress Your Best*.

ROB LONG is a writer and producer in Hollywood. He began his career writing and producing TV's long-running *Cheers*, and served as co-executive producer in its final season. He is a contributing editor of *National Review* and the *Los Angeles Times* and writes occasionally for the *Wall Street Journal* and the BBC *Radio Times* (UK). He is a cofounder of Ricochet.com, a website of center/right commentary.

MEGAN MCARDLE is the business and economics editor for *The Atlantic*. She has worked at three start-ups, a consulting firm, an investment bank, a disaster recovery firm at Ground Zero, and the *Economist*.

WILFRED M. MCCLAY is the SunTrust Chair of Excellence in Humanities at the University of Tennessee at Chattanooga. He is author of *The Masterless: Self and Society in Modern America*, which won the Merle Curti Award of the Organization of American Historians.

CAITRIN NICOL is managing editor of the *New Atlantis* and a writer living in Virginia. Her articles have appeared in *Commentary*, *First Things*, the *American Interest*, the *Weekly Standard*, and elsewhere. She holds a bachelor's degree from the University of Chicago.

JOE QUEENAN is the author of ten books, including *Balsamic Dreams: A Short but Self-Important History of the Baby Boomer Generation*. Queenan is a columnist for the weekend *Wall Street Journal* and a regular contributor to the *New York Times*, *Barron's*, the *Weekly Standard*, and the *Los Angeles Times*, a columnist for *Chief Executive*, and writes about pop culture for the *Guardian*.

NAOMI SCHAEFER RILEY is a former *Wall Street Journal* editor and writer whose work focuses on higher education, religion, philanthropy, and culture. She is the author of *God on the Quad: How Religious Colleges and the Missionary Generation Are Changing America* (St. Martin's, 2005) and *The Faculty Lounges . . . And Other Reasons That You Won't Get the College Education You Paid For* (Rowman and Littlefield, 2011). Ms. Riley's writings have appeared in the *Wall Street Journal*, the *New York Times*, the *Boston Globe*, the *L.A. Times*, and the *Chronicle of Higher Education* among other publications. She graduated magna cum laude from Harvard University in English and Government. She lives in the suburbs of New York with her husband, Jason, and their two children.

CHRISTINE ROSEN is senior editor of *The New Atlantis: A Journal of Technology & Society*, where she writes about the social impact of technology, bioethics, and the history of genetics. She is the author of *Preaching Eugenics: Religious Leaders and the American Eugenics Movement* (Oxford University Press, 2004), a history of the ethical and religious debates surrounding the eugenics movement in the United States, and *My Fundamentalist Education* (PublicAffairs, 2005), which tells the story of a Christian fundamentalist school in Florida. Mrs. Rosen has been an adjunct scholar at the American Enterprise Institute for Public Policy Research since 1999. Her essays and reviews have appeared in publications such as the *New York Times Magazine*, the *Wall Street Journal*, the *New Republic*, the *Washington Post*, the *American Historical Review*, the *Weekly Standard*, *Commentary*, the *New England Journal of Medicine*, the *Wilson Quarterly*, and *Policy Review*. She earned a B.A. in History from the University of South Florida in 1993, and a Ph.D. in History from Emory University in 1999. Mrs. Rosen lives in Washington, DC, with her husband, Jeffrey, and their children.

EMILY ESFAHANI SMITH is managing editor of the Hoover Institution journal *Defining Ideas* and an editor at the conservative blog Ricochet.com. A recent Dartmouth graduate, she was editor of the conservative newspaper, *The Dartmouth Review*. Author of the books *Oscar Wilde In An Hour* and *George Bernard Shaw In An Hour*, her writings have also appeared in the *Wall Street Journal*, the *Weekly Standard*, *The New Criterion*, the *American Spectator Online*, and *National Review Online*.

BRAD WALSH is a television writer and producer, who lives in Los Angeles with his family. Over the past fifteen years, Brad has written for shows on Fox, ABC, NBC, and CBS. He is currently a co-executive producer of ABC's *Modern Family*, for which he has won the Writers Guild award for Outstanding New Series as well as an Emmy award for Outstanding Comedy Series.

TONY WOODLIEF is a writer and management consultant whose essays have appeared in the *Wall Street Journal*, the *London Times*, *National Review*, and *WORLD Magazine*. His most recent book is the spiritual memoir *Somewhere More Holy*.